HC

2

Nations in Transition

HUNGARY

RAYMOND HILL

Facts On File, Inc.

Acknowledgments

The author wishes to thank Ms. Agnes Bodnar of the Hungarian Commercial Counselor's Office and Ms. Aniko Polgar of the Hungarian Tourist Board for their kind assistance in the gathering of information and photographs for this book. He also wishes to thank Mr. Joseph Magyar for agreeing to be interviewed by a complete stranger.

Hungary

Copyright © 1997 by Raymond Hill

Facts On File, Inc.
11 Penn Plaza
New York NY 10001

Library of Congress Cataloging-in-Publication Data

Hill, Raymond.
    Hungary / by Raymond Hill
        p.   cm. — (Nations in transition)
    Includes bibliographical references and index.
    ISBN 0-8160-3120-7 (alk. paper)
    1. Hungary—Juvenile literature. 2. Hungary. I. Title.
    II. Series.
    DB906.H45   1998
    943.9—DC20   95-32081

Facts On File books are available at special discounts when purchased in bulk quantities for businesses, associations, institutions or sales promotions. Please call our Special Sales Department in New York at 212/967-8800 or 800/322-8755.

Text design by Catherine Rincon Hyman
Cover design by Nora Wertz
MP FOF 10 9 8 7 6 5 4 3 2 1
This book is printed on acid-free paper.

Printed in the United States of America

Contents

Hungary

Introduction

A young woman who works in the Hungarian Tourist Board office in New York City spends much of her time answering questions on the telephone. The calls come from Americans who are thinking about vacationing in Hungary. The young woman, who has been in the United States for less than two years, tries to be as helpful as possible. She often marvels at how little Americans know about her native country.

"Sometimes they ask the strangest questions," she tells a visitor in accented but very good English. The visitor, himself an American, smiles encouragingly. "What kinds of questions?" he inquires.

"Well," she says, "they ask me: 'Does Hungary have roads?'" She shakes her head in amused dismay. (Yes, Hungary has quite a few roads.)

The young woman continues, "They ask me if they should bring their own food if they come to Hungary." The corners of her mouth twitch as she holds back a laugh. (No one goes hungry in Hungary. Getting a meal there is no problem. The country even has McDonald's.)

"And, they ask me: 'Where is Hungary?'" She cannot help laughing. Her visitor laughs with her.

The young woman composes herself and says seriously, "Americans do not know much about Hungary."

Her visitor agrees. "Most Americans," he tells her, "don't know much about anything that isn't American."

Hungary is a small country in the center of Europe. Hungarians like to say their country is in East-Central Europe. In pure geographic terms, it is in Central Europe. But if you factor in international politics, then Hungary is in Eastern Europe.

Confused? That response is only natural. Hungary right now is emerging from more than 40 years of Communist rule and domination by the Soviet Union. During the Cold War—the post–World War II period of tensions between the Communist nations and the Western democracies—Hungary had been part of the "Soviet bloc" (the nations in Central and Eastern Europe allied with the Soviet Union). The Soviet bloc also was known as the "Eastern bloc" because its member nations were located geographically east of the democracies of Western Europe. Hence, people in the West would say Hungary is in Eastern Europe.

Hungary still is in Eastern Europe in the sense that it has not yet shaken off the effects of Communist dictatorship. While it has made a smooth political transition to Western-style democracy, it is still struggling to transform its economic system to fit the Western mold. That means moving from a system in which the government completely controlled the economy to a system of market capitalism in which private enterprise is loosely regulated by the government. The two systems are worlds apart.

Before we speak further about the current transition, some useful facts are in order. Hungary is tiny in comparison to the United States. A motorist can travel from one end of the country to the other in about five hours without breaking any speed limits. Hungary's total area, which is slightly smaller than that of the state of Indiana, is 35,919 square miles. Its population, about 10.5 million, is less than that of the state of Illinois.

Hungary is a landlocked nation. Seven countries share its 1,407 miles of external borders: Austria on the west, Slovakia on northwest and north, Ukraine on the northeast, Romania on the east and southeast, Yugoslavia and Croatia on the south and Slovenia on the southwest.

Three important bodies of water mark Hungary's geography. The mighty Danube River forms part of the Slovak border and flows south through central Hungary to Yugoslavia, a journey of about 375 miles. East of the Danube, the smaller Tisza River runs from the northeast to Yugoslavia in the south. West of the Danube is Lake Balaton, the largest lake in Central Europe. Balaton is 50 miles long, 9 miles wide and occupies an area of 102 square miles.

Hungary's climate is usually mild, with a mean temperature of 50 degrees Fahrenheit (10 degrees Celsius). Winters tend to be damp, chilly and cloudy, with only moderate snowfalls. Summers tend to be warm and humid, but rarely are they oppressively hot. On average, Hungary gets about 25 inches of rain a year. The two main rivers, the Danube and Tisza, flood Hungary's flatlands nearly every year.

Hungary's most important natural resource is its rich, black soil. The earth has sustained Hungarian farmers for more than a thousand years. Wheat, corn, barley, sugar beets, potatoes and sunflowers are the nation's principal crops. About 57 percent of the country's land is used for growing crops, and about 14 percent for pasture for grazing livestock. Some 18 percent of Hungary is forest or woodland.

Hungary is blessed with large deposits of bauxite (the mineral that is processed into aluminum) and coal. Its mines also yield iron ore, copper and some gold and uranium.

The main ethnic group in Hungary is the Magyars, descendants of warrior horsemen from Central Asia. Magyars, with their unique language and culture, are very distinct from the Slavs and ethnic Germans that populate most of Hungary's neighboring nations. The predominance of Magyars means Hungarians are not so much Europeans as Europeanized Asians.

Magyars make up at least 90 percent of the population. An estimated 1 million Hungarians belong to minority groups. They include Gypsies, ethnic Germans, ethnic Slavs (Slovaks, Croats, Serbs and Ukrainians) and ethnic Romanians.

The official language of Hungary is Magyar. Many older Hungarians speak at least some German. Increasingly, young Hungarians are learning English as a second language. Magyar does not have its roots in the Indo-European languages that are predominant in Europe. Experts classify the language as an Ugro-Finnish language. It has some of the same traits as the Finnish and Estonian languages. There are 44 characters in the Hungarian alphabet, compared with 26 in the English alphabet. Names are reversed when written or spoken in the Hungarian language. Thus, Istvan Dobo Square in the city of Budapest is *Dobo Istvan ter* in Hungarian.

Although Hungary is primarily an agricultural country, 65 percent of its people live in cities and large towns. Hungary's capital, Budapest (population 2.9 million), is by far its largest city. Other large cities are Debrecen

A view of Budapest, Hungary's capital, taken from the Buda side of the Danube River. The domed parliament building in Pest is in the center, just across the river. (Hungarian Tourist Board)

(population about 214,700), Miskolc (about 191,600), Szeged (about 177,500), Pecs (about 169,500) and Gyoer (about 130,300).

Budapest, one of the world's most beautiful cities, is not only Hungary's political capital but also its economic and cultural center as well. The city was once three separate towns: Buda, Obuda and Pest. The Danube divides the hilly Buda from the flat Pest. (Looking south, in the direction of the flow of the river, Buda occupies the right bank and Pest the left bank.) Today, Obuda is a suburb of Buda.

Hungary is not alone in trying to make the difficult transition from communism to a free-market system. Poland, the Czech Republic, Slovakia and the other Eastern European countries are attempting to solve the same very tough problems. High unemployment, massive government debt, rising prices and feelings of uncertainty are only some of the costs of economic transition. So too are social unrest, mounting crime and a retreat into nationalism (an obsessive national self-interest).

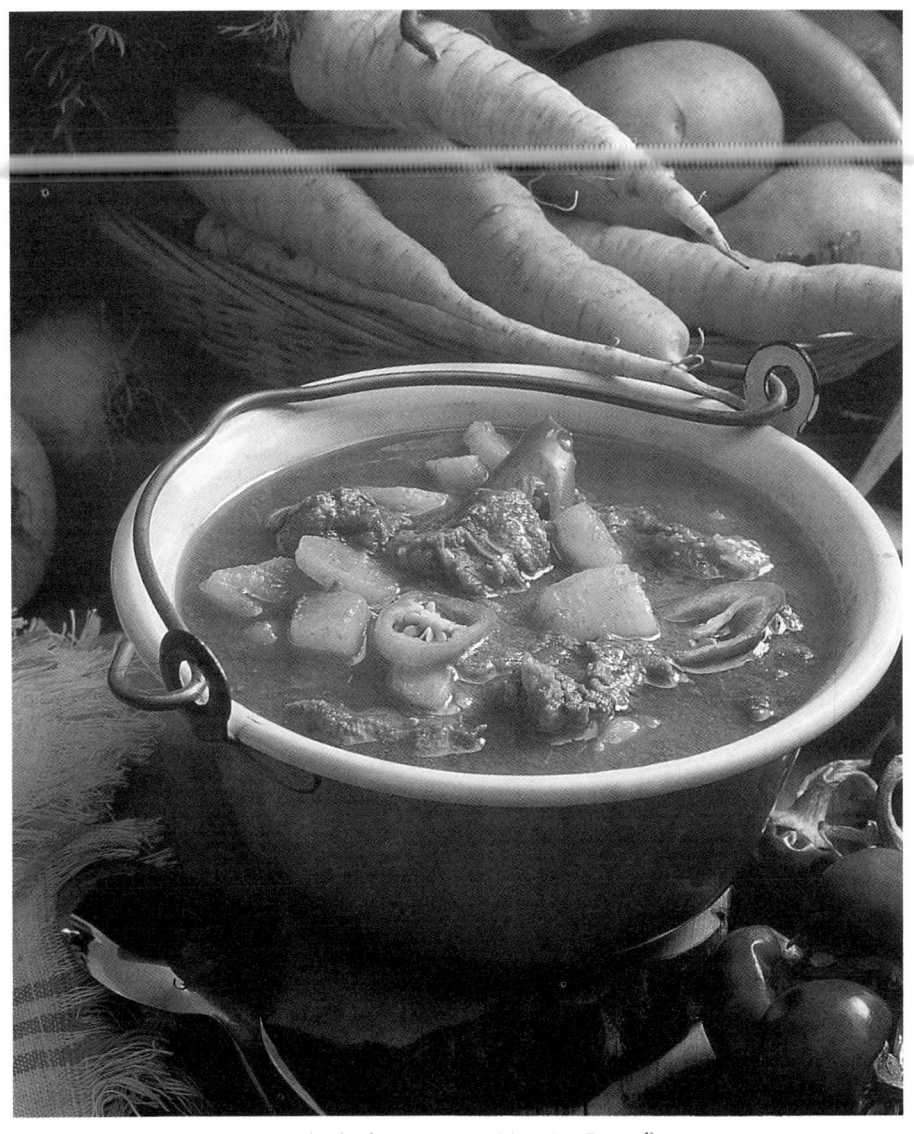

Authentic Hungarian goulash. (Hungarian Tourist Board)

This transformation, however, has not been all gloom and doom for Hungary. The country has received more foreign investment than any of its neighbors. Unlike the former Yugoslav states, Hungary is at peace. By and large, Hungarian workers are better paid now than ever before in the nation's history, and private enterprise, which is booming, has created an affluent middle class. More than 33 million tourists visit Hungary every year. (That is more than three times Hungary's population. Imagine 800 million tourists visiting the U.S. every year.)

Throughout this difficult period, Hungarians are taking heart in their proven ability to weather hard times. Although Hungary had been under foreign occupation of one sort or another for much of its long history, the country's culture, traditions and language have managed to survive, and even flourish.

The United States has existed for a little over 200 years. Hungary's history goes back 1,100 years. Yet, if the average Amercian hears the word "Hungary," he or she may think only of two things: goulash and the 1956 uprising.

Goulash is a meat stew that many non-Hungarians assume is Hungary's national dish. They are wrong; Hungary does not have a national dish. The goulash that became popular outside of Hungary in the late 1950s is not authentic. Authentic Hungarian goulash (*gulyas leves* in Hungarian) is more of a hearty soup than a stew.

The 1956 uprising, discussed in chapter 3, was a bloody, unsuccessful attempt by Hungary to break the chains of Soviet domination. It was a classic David-and-Goliath confrontation but, unlike in the Bible story, Goliath won. Hungary remained part of the Soviet empire until 1991.

Today, Hungarians mark the anniversary of the 1956 uprising with a national holiday (October 23). They know that the failed revolt resulted unexpectedly in a softer brand of communism—the West jokingly called it "goulash communism"—in Hungary. The new communism, in turn, undermined the entire Soviet bloc.

In some ways, the people of Hungary took revenge on the Soviets. With Hungary leading the way, the Eastern bloc fell apart and the Soviet Union itself collapsed.

Hungary's future is being decided at this moment, in the first decade of the transition from communism. This book will attempt to bring to the reader a sense of where the nation has been, where it is now, and where it is going.

PART I

HISTORY
OLD & NEW

Ninth Century to World War I

The Magyars Arrive

Late in the ninth century A.D., thousands of fierce horsemen swept westward through passes in the Carpathian Mountains of Central Europe and spread over the Carpathian Basin—the broad lowlands situated between the Carpathians and the Alps of South-Central Europe. The invaders were short and stocky, with black wavy hair that framed sun-weathered faces with dark eyes, high cheekbones and prominent noses. They rode strong, agile ponies—their most prized posses-sions—that were bred for both speed and endurance. The horsemen's favorite weapon was the bow, and they could shoot arrows with terrifying accuracy, even when riding their ponies at a thundering pace. They were the world's best mounted bowmen.

These were the Magyars, the ancestors of most modern-day Hungarians. They were a proud, independent people whose ancestry remains something of a mystery. Most historians believe the tribe originated somewhere in Central Asia and settled for a time in the foothills of the Ural Mountains of Russia. As early as the fourth century B.C., some Magyars were thought to have migrated to the Baltic coast of northern Europe and settled in areas that became the present-day nations of Finland and Estonia. That might explain why the Magyar language is loosely related to Finnish and Estonian.

The bulk of the Magyars left the Ural Mountains and wandered south and west to the Caspian Sea some time in the early seventh century A.D. More than a hundred years later, they left the Caspian region and pushed onto a steppe—or plain—north of the Black Sea. From the Black Sea region, the tribe moved northwards along the eastern flank of the Carpathian Mountains and then into Central Europe.

Throughout their wanderings, the Magyars encountered and mixed with other peoples. Hungarian historians are convinced that the Magyars were blood relatives of the Huns, a fierce Central Asian tribe that had terrorized Europe, and then returned to Asia, in the fifth century A.D. Also, it is likely that the Magyars interbred with the Khazars and other Turkic-speaking peoples of the Caspian Sea region.

Although little is known about the Magyars' social structure, historians believe the tribe was made up of seven clans, or sub-tribes, united by blood ties and customs. One observer, a ninth-century Arab trader, offered his impressions of the Magyars (whom he mistook for "Turks") in the Caspian Sea area. It was one of the first recorded sightings of the tribe:

> The Magyars are a race of Turks and their leader rides out with 20,000 horsemen. They have a plain which is all dry herbage and a wide territory . . . They have completely subjugated the Slavs, and they always order them to provide food for them and consider them as slaves. . . These Magyars are a handsome people and of good appearance, and their clothes are of silk brocade, and their weapons of silver encrusted with gold. They constantly plunder the Slavs.[1]

The Slavs in question were the ancestors of today's Russians. Through-out the eighth and ninth centuries there had also been a steady eastward migration of Slavic peoples to Russia from Central Europe. The Slavs were generally a peaceful folk who preferred farming, cattle-raising and trading over fighting. The Magyars—nomadic horse-breeders and warriors—no doubt felt crowded by the numerous Slav farms and villages that sprang up in the steppes of the Caspian region. It was their need for wide-open spaces, more than any other factor, that most likely forced the Magyars to leave the area.

Under a powerful leader named Arpad, the seven clans migrated south and west. Their destination, a plain north of the Black Sea, turned out to be only a temporary stop. There the Magyars encountered the Pechengs, a warlike Turkic tribe that was already established in the area. Unlike the passive Caspian Slavs, the Pechengs offered fierce resistance to the intruding Magyars. The Magyars chose to move on. They crossed the Carpathian Mountains and descended into the Carpathian Basin in the winter of 895–96.

The Terrors of Europe

The Carpathian Basin was far from uninhabited when the Magyars arrived. A thousand years earlier, it had been sparsely settled by Asiatic tribesmen known as Scythians. Then there had been successive waves of other settlers: Celts from Northwest Europe, Avars (a nomadic Asian tribe), Romans and Slavs. The Romans—who had one of the great empires of the ancient world—established a large colony in West-Central Europe in the first century A.D. The Roman colony—called Pannonia—encompassed what is today western Hungary, lower Austria and Croatia. The Slavs cohabited the region with the Romans from the third century A.D. until the fifth century, when the invading Huns pushed out the Romans. After the Huns returned to Asia, Germanic tribes dominated the northern part of the basin, but the rest of the area was Slavic.

After descending the Carpathian Mountains, the Magyars moved south and set up a settlement on the site of the current northeastern Hungarian town of Eger. From there, they rode through the Great Plain, the vast *puszta* (grasslands) of eastern Hungary, which in those days contained some forests. The plain—which resembled the Russian steppes—was much to the liking of the horsemen, who spread throughout the region, establishing settlements along the way.

Late in 896, Magyar clan chieftains gathered on the site of what is today the town of Szeged, in south-central Hungary, and pledged loyalty to their king, Arpad. According to legend, the chieftains sealed their pledge by drinking from goblets filled with human blood. Europeans were more than willing to believe the grisly legend, given the Magyars bloodthirsty ways.

The Slavs were the first residents of the basin to find out the Magyars were bad neighbors. The Slavs were a collection of separate tribes that shared a common language and culture. The Carpathian Basin was the hub of the Slavic world. It was there that the lands of the Western Slavs (Moravians, Bohemians [Czechs], Slovaks and Poles) converged with the lands of the Southern Slavs (Serbs, Croats and Slovenes). When the Magyars arrived, they cut off the Western Slavs from their southern kinsmen. That division would have repercussions into the 20th century.

One of the earliest Slav states, the kingdom of Greater Moravia, had been created by the Western Slavs in the seventh century and reached its height early in the ninth century. Greater Moravia included the regions that now form modern Austria and Croatia. But the heart of the kingdom was the lands of Bohemia, Moravia and Slovakia. (Today, Bohemia and Moravia form the Czech Republic. Slovakia, on Hungary's northern border, is now the Republic of Slovakia.)

Unfortunately for the Slavs, the kingdom was in decline when the Magyars arrived. The Magyar horde invaded Greater Moravia in 896, and soon afterward defeated the kingdom's forces in a battle fought near Bratislava (the capital of modern Slovakia). The horsemen overran most of the kingdom with the notable exceptions of the territories of Moravia and Bohemia, these states having been brought under the protection of some German states.

As in the Caspian region, the warrior Magyars regarded the relatively civilized Slavs as weak and inferior. The Slavs in the occupied remnants of Greater Moravia became the slaves of the Magyars. Those Slavs not taken directly into bondage were made to pay tribute—in the form of gold, food crops, cattle and young women—to their new masters.

The Slavs were not the only Europeans to suffer at the hands of the Magyars. Beginning in 896 and for the next 60 years, the Magyars were the terror of the continent. From their camps in the Carpathian Basin, they launched massive hit-and-run raids that carried thousands of horsemen as far west as France and as far south as Italy. The mounted bowmen struck towns, villages and Christian monasteries, looting, raping and killing with barbaric glee. Their deadly rain of arrows easily defeated the small armed forces that opposed them. Larger forces declined to pursue the Magyars because the horsemen, while retreating at full speed, would turn around in their saddles and fire arrows at any riders who dared to chase them.

The sound of thundering hooves and the alarm, "The Magyars are coming!" was enough to make trembling villagers throughout Europe cram into their churches and pray for mercy. According to British historian Rowlinson Carter:

> To Europe, the Magyars were savages, barely human in character and interested only in rape and plunder . . . Their arrival was interpreted as a sign that the Day of Judgment was at hand.[2]

To the Magyars, Europe was one great treasure chest of booty. The marauders returned from their raids with stolen gold, silver, horses, cattle, weapons, rich cloth, wealthy hostages for ransoming, and young women. Captured women were forced to bear children by Magyar men and thus increase the tribe's population.

During their raiding period, which lasted until the middle of the 10th century, people began referring to the Magyars as "Hungarians." However, many Hungarians believe that the name, which can be translated literally as "those from the land of the Huns," comes from the fact that the Huns had launched their ferocious attack on Europe in the fifth century from the same area later occupied by the Magyars. (To this day, the townspeople of Szeged, Hungary, boast that the Huns' fearsome and famous leader Attila once had his headquarters on the site of the town.) Historians differ on the matter, with some holding that the word "Hungarian" is probably derived from the Onogurs, a prominent Magyar clan. At any rate, the Magyars were widely known as "Hungarians" by the end of the 10th century. Today, the Hungarian word *Magyar* translates into English as "Hungarian."

Defeat and Christianization

At its height, the empire established by Charlemagne (742–814), a German, in 800 A.D. in alliance with the powerful Roman Catholic Church, included most of western and northern Europe and parts of southern Europe. But internal bickering and political intrigues had weakened and divided the empire to the point that it was a mere shadow of its former self when the Magyars appeared.

By the tenth century, North-Central Europe was dominated by a collection of feuding German principalities that included Saxony, Prussia, Bavaria, and Austria. These German states made up the eastern portion of the crumbling Carolingian Empire, or Empire of the West, the Christian successor to the former Roman Empire.

One mission of Charlemagne's successors was to hold back the encroachment of the Eastern Orthodox religion, which rivaled the Roman Catholic Church. The Slavs made up the bulk of Eastern Orthodox worshipers in Europe. The German states helped to contain the spread of the Slavs and their religion from the Carpathian Basin. When the Magyars invaded the basin, the Slavs lost all hope of pushing any farther into Europe than they already had.

From Germania's perspective, the Magyars themselves were the problem. The Germans regarded the newcomers as dangerous, godless savages who had to be subdued at all costs. One German prince in particular, Otto I, managed to rally the German states to fight the horsemen from the East.

The Magyars were experts in raiding, but never before had confronted large, organized armies on open battlefields. They were unfamiliar with the systematic rules of warfare that had evolved in Europe. Consequently, forces under Otto I routed the Magyars at the Battle of Augsburg (also known as the Battle of Lechfeld), in Germany, in 955. Otto was crowned emperor of a newly established Holy Roman Empire in 962.

The Battle of Augsburg all but ended the Magyar raids. The tribesmen settled down to consolidate the territories they still held, which were still considerable. Magyar territories included all of Slovakia, a sliver of northeastern Croatia, part of northern Serbia, part of what is today Ukraine, and Transylvania, now part of Romania. The wealthiest Magyars in these regions had large landholdings. Slavs formed the core of slave labor on these holdings.

The Magyars were wary of the Holy Roman Empire, but they were also fascinated by the Germans' social structure, culture and religion. The Germans, like the rest of the more refined parts of Europe, were evolving a feudal social structure. In such a structure, the king was on top, nobles in the middle and the poorest classes, peasants and slaves, on the bottom.

Little is known about the Magyar religion. They were most certainly some sort of pagans, in that they probably did not worship a single deity. Perhaps, like other nomadic horsemen, they worshiped natural elements, like the wind. German Catholic missionaries found willing converts among the Magyar nobles. More and more, missionaries began to appear at the side of Magyar leaders.

The Crown of St. Stephen

Geza, the great-grandson of Arpad, the leader who had led the tribe to its new home, converted to Christianity in the year 972. Geza's son Stephen (977–1038) ordered all Magyars to adopt the religion, and even invited the Vatican (the center of the Roman Catholic religion located in Rome, Italy) to send priests to help convert all his people. Stephen took his religion seriously. Any Magyar who disobeyed his order to convert was buried alive, along with his family and beloved horses. Still, there were some who resisted the idea of giving up the old ways in favor of a "love-thy-neighbor" religion.

Bishop Gerard, an Italian, came to Hungary to observe the progress of the mass conversion. He preached to a crowd at the top of a 770-foot hill in the town of Buda, overlooking the Danube River. It is not known what he said to the Magyars, but he apparently angered a number of people. The bishop met a terrible fate after his speech. As recounted by travel writer Phyllis Meras: "Some of those who did not wish to be Christianized captured him, tied him to a barrel studded with nails, and rolled him off [the] hill into the Danube."[3]

The unfortunate bishop was canonized as St. Gerard. Hungarians know him as St. Gellert (the Magyar version of Gerard). A statue of him converting pagans stands atop that fatal Budapest hill, now known as Gellert Hill.

Murdered bishop aside, the Vatican was encouraged by the conversion efforts in Hungary. Pope Sylvester II was so grateful that he appointed Stephen an apostle of the church and crowned him a Christian king on Christmas Day in the year 1000. King Stephen established a strong Roman Catholic tradition in Hungary, and the church declared him a saint after his death. Stephen's crown, formally called the Holy Apostolic Crown, is the centerpiece of Hungary's royal jewels. Since his death, Hungarian monarchs were said to wear the "Crown of St. Stephen."

King Stephen's contributions were not only in the realm of religion. He married a German noblewoman to solidify ties between Hungary and Germania. From his seat of government in Gran (today's town of Esztergom), he handed down Hungary's first written laws and had the Magyars adopt the trappings of European civilization. He brought scholars from all over the continent to teach and study in Hungary. He invited artists and craftspeople to settle in Hungary and pass along their creative skills to the Magyars.

Stephen also established a social order that placed all Magyars, no matter how poor, over non-Magyars. Non-Magyars fell into two categories: those who had been in the Carpathian Basin when the Magyars arrived, and those who came to Hungary as "guests and immigrants." Of those guests and immigrants, according to British historian Carter:

> Many were Germans (lumped together misleadingly as "Saxons"), a mixture of knights, miners, artisans and town-dwellers. There also were Jewish merchants ("Ishmaelites"), Moslem Bulgars (in charge of the royal mint) and Slavs who were often invited to settle in waste land or forest and bring on cultivation. Foreign nobles who entered Hungary were invariably given the equivalent of Hungarian rank and status.[4]

Stephen's descendants were neither as wise nor as strong as he was. The Magyar nobles nearly revolted against King Andras II after he plundered the royal treasury and sold off royal lands to support an extravagant lifestyle. The pope had to step in and act as a mediator. The result was the Papal Bull (document) of 1222. It effectively ended the monarchy's absolute power over the Magyar nobility.

The Mongols, who were Asiatic horsemen much like the old Magyars, invaded Hungary in 1241 and wiped out nearly half the population. King

The Hungarian crown jewels: the Holy Apostolic Crown of St. Stephen (top center), the Royal Scepter of Power (right), the Golden Collar (bottom), orb with pontifical cross, and St. Stephen's sword. (Wide World Photos)

Bela IV led an army against them at the Battle of Mohi, and he barely escaped when the Mongols annihilated the Magyar forces. The invaders reached the royal capital, the town of Pest, across the Danube from Buda, and burned it to the ground. King Bela learned a crucial lesson: never build your capital on low ground. He moved the royal court across the river to the more defensible high ground of the Buda Hills. The Mongols did not stay in Hungary for long. Internal political conflicts in their Asian homeland compelled them to leave Europe.

Power-hungry nobles murdered King Andras III in 1301, ending a long line of monarchs descended from King Arpad. The nobles put a Frenchman, Louis of Anjou, on the Hungarian throne. After Louis, the Crown of St. Stephen passed to several other foreigners. One was

Matyas Hunyadi, a Romanian, who defeated an invading Turkish army at Belgrade (the current capital of Yugoslavia) in 1377. Another was Matyas' son, who was known as Matthias Corvinus (Latin for crow, from a heraldic symbol on his family's coat of arms), who died in 1490.

Corvinus ruled from 1458 to 1490. During his reign, Hungary was the strongest, richest and most admired country in Central Europe, and Buda was a center for scholars and artists. He established Hungary's first library, the Corvina. During his reign, advantageous marriages between Hungarian royals and the members of other royal families gave Hungary part of lower Austria, all of Moravia, and Silesia (now part of Poland).

There is suspicion that Corvinus was poisoned, perhaps by jealous nobles. After his death, the country was beset by disputes over succession and by serious internal disorders. There was a bloody peasant uprising in 1514 and the Turks once again moved against the country's borders. Hungary got no help from the Holy Roman Empire. The Germans were too busily engaged in a feud with the papacy to offer any assistance.

Hapsburg Domination Begins

A Turkish army of Sultan Suleiman II, the Magnificent, crushed the Hungarian army under King Louis II at the historic Battle of Mohacs on August 29, 1526. Louis had led an army of about 20,000 against a Turkish force numbering 200,000 and was drowned while trying to retreat across a river.

Louis II had been married to noblewomen of the Hapsburg family, the powerful dynasty centered in Austria. With Louis' defeat, the Crown of St. Stephen eventually passed into the hands of his Hapsburg in-laws. Hungary would remain under Austrian domination for the next 462 years.

Nearly all of Hungary was occupied by the sultan's forces but for two notable exceptions. One was the Principality of Transylvania, whose Magyar nobility avoided absorption by paying tribute to the Turks. The other was called "Royal Hungary," a small area in what is now Slovakia.

The Turks held Hungary in an oppressive grip for 150 years, imposed crushing taxes on the populace, built mosques (Moslem places of worship) in Hungarian towns, and converted many Christian churches into mosques. They cut down the forests of the Great Plain to prevent Magyar rebels from having a place to hide, but the people were determined to keep their language and customs alive. Most Magyars staunchly resisted pressure to convert to Islam. (That was not true in other parts of Turkish-occupied Europe. In Bosnia-Herzegovina, south of Hungary, many Slavs converted, which is why today the majority of Bosnians are Moslems.)

Most of Hungary's aristocracy fled to Royal Hungary and Transylvania during the Turkish occupation. The peasants remained, but they were probably no worse off under the Turks than they had been under the Magyars.

Hungary's aristocracy had to rely on the armies of Austria to gradually push the Turks out. That was accomplished by 1697. The Turks left two enduring legacies. One was paprika, a pepper that Hungarians use to season many of their dishes. The other legacy was Turkish baths. Today, attending baths and spas is a regular social ritual in Hungary.

In return for the Austrians' help, Hungary was compelled to accept the rule of the Hapsburgs. For one thing, only the powerful Austrians could

The town of Eger boasts the oldest Moslem mosque in Europe, built by the Turks in the 16th century. Its minaret (prayer tower) is in the foreground. (Wide World Photos)

return order to Hungary. Land ownership was in dispute. The rural middle class (owners of small landholdings) and peasants resented a return of the Magyar aristocracy.

The Magyars chafed under the thumb of the Hapsburg Empire until 1724, when the Hapsburg crown passed to Empress Maria Theresa. Austria was threatened with an invasion of joint Bavarian and French forces, and much of the Austrian army refused to fight because it had not been paid for some time. History tells us that Maria, mounted on a white horse and clutching her newborn son, made a dramatic appeal to Hungarians for help. The six regiments (about 6,000 troops) of loyal Hungarians that rallied to her banner played a key role in halting the invaders, Maria Theresa was forever grateful to Hungary. Hungary, in turn, recognized the empress as its legitimate ruler. She was the only woman ever to wear the Crown of St. Stephen.

Joseph II, the son of Maria Theresa, had little regard for Hungary. He refused to wear the royal crown. He taxed Hungary's aristocrats (something no monarch had done since 1222), and he attempted to put an end to Hungarian feudalism. The Hapsburgs wanted to shape Hungary in Austria's image: a highly centralized and bureaucratic government structure coupled with a fledgling industrial economy. The foundation of Hungary's political and economic power lay in its great rural estates.

About 200 aristocratic families, and 3,000 wealthy but untitled families, owned nearly half of the arable land in Hungary. The Roman Catholic Church also held vast tracts of land. Although some members of the peasant class earned viable livings as farmers (the so-called smallholders—owners of up to 130 acres each), most peasants lived in or on the edge of poverty.

The majority of Hungarian peasants were landless. They lived in villages on the great estates and endured lives of hardship only a step above slavery. (The Austrians ended slavery in Hungary in the 18th century.) Under ancient tradition and law, they were bound for life to work for the landowning elite. The landowners had the right to punish any peasant who attempted to leave the land. Other peasants worked as itinerant farm laborers. They moved from estate to estate, cultivating the soil and picking crops for subsistence wages.

Hungary's Magyar population in the mid-1800s was 5.5 million. Due to the acquisition of outlying territories, the Magyars were far out-numbered by other ethnic groups that were part of the kingdom of St. Stephen. These included over 2 million Romanians, and over a million each of Slovaks, Germans, Serbs and Croats. There were also ethnic Ukrainians, ethnic Slovenes and others.

The ethnic minorities (who together constituted a majority) were content to maintain their own languages and customs, just as the Magyars resisted Austrian influence. But in 1843 Magyar was declared the official language of Hungary and all Hungarian territories. It was the first act of "Magyarization," or the policy of forcing other ethnic groups to adhere to Magyar culture. The policy would inspire separatist movements in the lands under Hungarian rule that would be active for more than 70 years.

Revolution and Absolutism

Nationalist and political unrest brewed in Hungary and throughout Europe in the mid-1800s, inspired in part by concepts first introduced in the French Revolution of 1789. One concept held that no nationality or ethnic group had a right to rule another. Another held that, within a given country, citizens were entitled to a truly representative government, not one controlled by monarchs or aristocrats. Both of these concepts played a role in the Hungarian Revolution of 1848–49. First, most Hungarians wished to be rid of Austrian rule. Second, many of the key figures in the revolution supported moves toward democracy.

Count Istvan Szechenyi and Lajos Kossuth were two figures who sought broad social changes in Hungary. Szechenyi, although an aristocrat, called for sweeping reforms, including universal suffrage and education for Hungary's illiterate masses. Kossuth, a left-wing lawyer, swayed intellectuals and radical politicians with demands for independence from Austria and for an end to feudalism.

Austria's Emperor Ferdinand I sought to defuse the situation by making concessions. In 1847, he granted Hungary limited autonomy, created a Hungarian diet (parliament) and allowed limited voting rights. In order to be eligible to vote, Hungarians had to own property and have some education. Count Lajos Batthanyi became Hungary's first elected premier, and he appointed Szechenyi and Kossuth to cabinet posts.

Armed friction between Magyars and independence-minded ethnic Romanians, Croats and Serbs (among others), however, brought requests in Austria for a tougher stance toward the unruly Hungary. Ferdinand abdicated the Hapsburg throne in 1848 and he was succeeded by his young nephew Francis Joseph (1830–1916).

The new emperor rejected Ferdinand's more tolerant approach toward the Hungarian people. He ordered nothing less than Hungary's absolute obedience to the Hapsburg monarchy. The order precipitated a nationalist revolt in Hungary in 1848 led by Kossuth. In April 1849, the Hungarian diet declared an independent Hungarian republic with Kossuth as its "governor."

Hungary's hastily recruited "revolutionary army" defeated Austrian imperial troops in several skirmishes, but the success was to be short-lived. A humiliated Francis Joseph appealed to czarist Russia for help and in

A Poem by Sandor Petoefi (1823–1849)

Sandor Petoefi was the poet of the 1848–49 Hungarian Revolution against Hapsburg Austrian rule. He was a Magyar patriot and a democrat. Petoefi not only despised the emperor of Austria, he hated all monarchs. Here is one of his poems:

A knife in the heart of Lamberg,* a rope around the neck of Latour,*
And after them others may follow;
You begin to be mighty, O people!
This is all right, this is perfectly fine,
But this has achieved little.
Hang the kings.

---
*High-ranking Austrian government officials in 1848, at the start of the revolution

Matthias Church in Budapest, where Austrian Emperor Francis Joseph was crowned king of Hungary in 1867.
(Hungarian Tourist Board)

May 1849, Russian troops entered the fray. Together, Austria and Russia put nearly 300,000 soldiers in the field. The small, badly equipped Hungarian revolutionary army was overwhelmed. The ragtag insurgents, under General Artur Gorgey, surrendered to the Russians on August 13, 1849, at the village of Vilagos, Hungary. Kossuth and several other members of the revolutionary government fled to Turkey. Premier Batthanyi was captured and executed.

There followed 18 years of Austrian absolute rule in Hungary, which had the status of a "royal land." In effect, Hungary was the emperor's personal property. Francis Joseph divided the non-Magyar lands into four separate administrative regions of Austria: Transylvania, Croatia, Slovenia and Vojvodina (northern Serbia). Austria took Moravia from Hungary.

During this period of absolutism, Hungary had no parliament. It was ruled by a governor-general, Prince Felix Schwarzenberg, who filled the government bureaucracy with Germans and Czechs. Hungary's police forces were run by another Austrian, Interior Minister Alexander Bach. The so-called Bach era was characterized by the brutal treatment of any Hungarians suspected of harboring nationalist tendencies.

The Hapsburgs made German the official language of Hungary. Hungarians were barred from using their native language in government offices, courts and schools. In addition, Hungarians were stripped of all civil rights. Austrian officials confiscated Hungarian property without hearings, and thousands of Hungarians suspected of revolutionary activities were jailed without trial.

Amid the simmering discontent, a Magyar tailor's apprentice, Janos Libenyi, attempted to kill Francis Joseph with a knife on a Vienna street in 1853. He failed—the emperor was wounded but recovered—and Libenyi was executed.

The Dual Monarchy

While holding Hungary in an iron grip, the Austrian Empire fared badly in wars against Italy, France and Prussia. Relations with Russia deteriorated. The setbacks helped convince Emperor Francis Joseph of the wisdom of consolidating the empire. He accepted a petition from a group of Hungarian moderate nationalists, led by Ferenc Deak, to restore Hungary's autonomy under a unique framework—the Dual Monarchy.

Modern soldiers re-create the Austro-Hungarian era by dressing in uniforms similar to those of the 19th-century Hungarian cavalry. (Wide World Photos)

The Compromise of 1867 made Francis Joseph the king of Hungary as well as the emperor of a combined Austro-Hungarian Empire. Austria and Hungary each had its own elected parliament and separate government. The important areas of defense, finance and foreign relations were handled by the consensus agreement of representatives from both parts of the empire. Issues such as trade and commerce between Austria and Hungary were governed by renewable 10-year agreements. Hungary regained its non-Magyar territories with the exception of the Czech lands, which were held by Austria.

Austria did not allow heavy concentrations of Hungarian troops in Hungary. Those forces were dispersed throughout the empire. Austria based Croat troops in Hungary. Although Slavs, Croat men regarded service in the Austrian military to be an honor. On the other hand, the Croats had an intense dislike for Magyars, partly because of the arrogant rule of the Magyars in Slavonia (northeastern Croatia). The basing of Croat soldiers in Hungary was not accidental.

Francis Joseph was one of the craftiest political thinkers of the day. He held the empire together by continually playing one ethnic element against another. The groups were too busy fighting each other to notice who was pulling the strings. In a conversation with the French ambassador in Vienna, the emperor disclosed:

> My people are all estranged from one another and this is all for the good. . . . I send the Magyars to Italy and the Italians to Hungary. Each of them watches his neighbor; they do not understand each other and they hate each other. Out of their mistrust order is born and from their mutual hatred a lasting peace arises.[5]

The Dual Monarchy was fully supported by Hungary's two most powerful classes, the landowning aristocrats and the middle-class farmers. There remained an undercurrent of anti-Austria feeling in Hungary, but the only organized opposition came from the 48 Party (later renamed the Independence Party), a leftist organization that drew its inspiration from Lajos Kossuth, the revolutionary hero.

Hungary's dominant political organization during the Dual Monarchy was the Liberal Party. Its platform, a mixture of moderate left-center nationalism and a desire to maintain the social status quo, was popular with the upper and middle classes.

Until World War I, the empire was stable and relatively prosperous. Hungary accounted for almost half of the empire's agricultural production. There was steady industrialization in Hungary during the last half of the 19th century. More and more people moved to the cities. By the early 1900s, the percentage of agricultural workers in the total work force had declined from 75 percent to 60 percent.

Conditions in Hungary's factories were harsh. Workers labored for long hours at low pay. Women and children made up about three-fifths of all factory workers. However, for unskilled laborers, life in the cities and large towns was better than the dawn-to-dusk drudgery of laboring on the large estates.

A new urban middle class appeared in Hungary, made up mostly of Jews who had emigrated to Hungary from Russia, Poland and other Slavic countries. Due to a tolerant atmosphere in Hungary's cities, Jews thrived as business owners, bankers, financiers, lawyers, doctors, teachers and government bureaucrats. Jews formed about 4.5 percent of the population in 1910 (932,000). Most of Hungary's larger cities had at least a 12 percent Jewish population. Prior to World War I, Budapest was 23 percent Jewish.

Educational opportunities also expanded under the Dual Monarchy. Improvements in basic education reduced the illiteracy rate from 77 percent in 1867 to about 41 percent in 1914. Although the poorest Hungarians rarely received higher education, there was a sharp increase in university attendance among the wealthy and middle classes. In the mid-1800s, there were only about 800 university students in Hungary. By 1914, the number increased to over 16,000.

Cultural nationalism, a romantic attachment to all things Magyar, also flourished during the Dual Monarchy. The writings of Zsigmond Moricz and Endre Ady, the plays of Ferenc Molnar and the musical works of composers such as Franz Liszt, Bela Bartok and Zoltan Kodaly were lionized.

While Austria-Hungary was a model of stability, the political situation in the rest of the Balkan region was not. (The region, encompassing Southeast Europe, has long been a volatile area. Hungary occupies the northernmost part of the Balkan region.) At the turn of the century, the empire was increasingly at odds with the Kingdom of Serbia. The Serbs wished to unite with Hungary's Serbs, Croats and Slovenes to form a southern Slav kingdom. Russia was Serbia's ally and protector.

Two Balkan wars were fought in 1912–13. In the first, Serbia, Bulgaria, Greece and Montenegro pushed the remnants of the Turkish Ottoman Empire out of Europe. In the second, Bulgaria attacked Serbia, but was defeated when Romania, Greece and Turkey came to Serbia's aid. Austria-Hungary was not involved in the Balkan Wars, but the proximity of the conflicts made Francis Joseph nervous. In casting about for allies against Serbia and Russia, he moved diplomatically closer to Germany.

A big war was looming in Europe. It was triggered on June 28, 1914, when a radical Serb student, Gavrilo Princip, assassinated the heir apparent to the Austrian throne, Archduke Francis Ferdinand, in the Bosnian capital of Sarajevo.

Hungary had nothing to do with the assassination, but at first some Austrians suspected that Magyars were behind the plot. That is because Archduke Francis Ferdinand hated Magyars, whom he viewed as treacherous. The archduke, who was very unpopular in Hungary, made no secret of his bias. While the Austrian press was barred from openly criticizing the Hapsburg royal family, the Hungarian press frequently mocked the archduke as a fool and a bigot. Here Francis Ferdinand rails in a letter to the German leader, Kaiser Wilhelm:

> The so-called gentlemanly Magyar is a most infamous, antidynastic, lying, unreliable fellow. . . . All the difficulties which we have in the Monarchy arise exclusively from the Magyars.[6]

Following the assassination, the Central Powers—Austria-Hungary and its ally, Germany—declared war on Serbia. The Allies—Russia, Britain and France—came to Serbia's aid. World War I had begun.

Hungary's Liberal premier, Count Istvan Tisza, doubted the Central Powers could win. At first he sought to avoid Hungarian involvement in the conflict, but then reluctantly relented. Hungary could not sit out the war while Austria—its partner in the Dual Monarchy—took part. Tisza publicly disavowed the notion that Hungary had territorial designs on Serbia or any other neighbor. As it turned out, Hungary would be the one to lose most of its territory to its neighbors when the war ended.

NOTES

1. Rowlinson Carter, *Insight Guides: Eastern Europe* (Singapore: APA Publications [HK] Ltd., 1993), p. 238.
2. Ibid.
3. Phyllis Meras, *Eastern Europe: A Traveler's Guide* (Boston: Houghton Mifflin Co., 1991), p. 209.
4. Rowlinson, p. 239.
5. Vladimir Dedijer, *The Road to Sarajevo* (New York: Simon and Schuster, Inc., 1966), p. 118.
6. Ibid., p. 136.

2

World War I Through World War II 1918–45)

The Great War

World War I was fought between 1914 and 1918 and resulted in over eight million deaths, both to soldiers and civilians. It was mainly a conflict between two major European power blocs: the Allies (Great Britain, France and Russia) and the Central Powers (Germany and Austria-Hungary). The United States entered the war in 1917 and helped speed the Allied victory. At stake in the conflict was domination of global economic markets, although American president Woodrow Wilson viewed the outcome as a triumph of the forces of democracy over the forces of tyranny.

The First World War was the catalyst of Hungary's independence from Austria. But Hungary was on the losing side of the war, and as such received drastic punishment from the Allies.

Hungarians generally were enthusiastic about the First World War when it began. Magyars viewed the conflict as a means of punishing Russia for its role in smashing the Hungarian revolt of 1848–49. The kingdom's loyal Slavs regarded themselves as Hungarians first and foremost, and therefore were willing to fight their ethnic cousins in Serbia and Russia. Nationalist Slavs knew enough to be patient, believing that they would eventually win their freedom regardless of the war's outcome.

The leaders of the Austro-Hungarian Empire had visions of regaining its past glory, but it was too weak militarily to have more than a secondary role in the Central Power alliance. Germany planned the overall war strategy, and German troops did the bulk of the fighting against French and British forces on the all-important Western Front (the fighting in France and Belgium). Hungarians mainly fought on the Eastern Front, where the kingdom's principal military role was to defend the many passes in the Carpathian Mountains against advances by Serbian and Russian troops.

Premier Tisza turned the entire Hungarian economy toward support of the war. Farmers, miners and industrial workers labored around the clock to produce raw materials, weapons and food for the Central Powers. Calls for political, social and economic reforms were set aside in the name of national unity.

Hungarian forces suffered heavy losses in the early years of the conflict, but the fact that Hungary itself was under a real threat of invasion from the east helped to fuel patriotic spirit. Hungarian troops played a pivotal part in the Central Powers' capture and occupation of Serbia, in 1915, and Montenegro, south of Serbia, in 1916. However, the conflict dragged into 1916 with no end in sight, and Hungary's population grew increasingly weary of the war. The kingdom's economy had been drained by supporting the war effort. Civilians were worn down by the exhaustive work schedules, food shortages and soaring prices for goods.

Germany unwittingly contributed to a growing discontent in Hungary. Hungarians resented Germany's arrogant leadership of the Central Powers. German propaganda, which characterized the war as a "Germanic" crusade against "Slavdom," not only ignored Magyar sacrifices in the war, but trampled on sensitivities of the loyal Slavs in Hungary. On the other hand, the Allies actively encouraged Slavic nationalism in Hungary's territories, prompting some Hungarian military units to stage mass desertions to the Allied side.

The political unity of 1914–15 fell apart. A new Hungarian Independence Party (actually a splinter faction of the old Independence Party) was formed in the summer of 1916 by the reform-minded leader Count Mihaly Karolyi. The party defied Tisza's ruling Liberal government by calling for Hungary to end its participation in the war and focus attention on internal reforms. The Independentce Party began to gather widespread support as the war continued and defeat loomed for the empire.

Emperor Francis Joseph, the Hapsburg monarch since 1848, died in November 1916 at the age of 86. King Charles IV of Hungary succeeded Francis Joseph on the dual throne, taking the title Emperor Charles I of Austria-Hungary. Charles realized that Germany was leading the Central Powers to defeat. He quietly—and unsuccessfully—sought a separate peace with the Allies, hoping to salvage the empire.

Peace protests and work stoppages hit the empire in 1917, compelling Emperor Charles to place the most important sectors of the Austro-Hungarian economy under the control of the military. Charles dismissed Hungarian Premier Tisza in May 1917 following a massive antiwar demonstration in Budapest. (Tisza would be murdered by disgruntled Hungarian soldiers in 1918.) The new premier, Sandor Werkele (who had held the post twice before), could do little to halt the unrest. Left-wing movements sprang up throughout Hungary, denouncing the war and demanding democratic reforms. The government cracked down on reformers, jailing as many of the leaders as they could find. But the reform movements had already gained wide support among urban workers throughout the empire.

A strike by munitions workers, first in Austria and then spreading to Hungary, paralyzed the empire's production lines in January 1918 and finally ended through army intervention. Army units mutinied in May 1918 in the Hungarian city of Pecs. The mutiny was put down bloodily by loyal army units.

In June 1918, Hungarian workers staged a nine-day nationwide general strike. The government responded by declaring martial law. Only mediation by the Social Democratic Party convinced the strikers to return to their jobs. Slavic nationalists took advantage of the chaos by asking the Allies to recognize formally their right to independence from the empire. In the summer of 1918, the Allies recognized the Czech National Council as the true representative of the Czech people. The South Slav and Romanian National Councils also gained Allied recognition.

In October 1918, a month before the end of World War I, Hungary experienced a massive political upheaval. Charles I issued a manifesto on October 16 that declared Austria-Hungary's willingness to end its participation in the war. The same day, Hungarian premier Wekerle proposed an end of the Dual Monarchy, with Austria and Hungary to function as separate nations. Neither the manifesto nor the proposal addressed the issues of Slav independence or far-reaching reforms in Hungary.

Wekerle resigned as premier October. 23, 1918. On October 25, the Independence Party, Social Democratic Party and leading left-wing movements announced the formation of an opposition front called the Hungarian National Council. The council issued a 12-point program calling for an immediate separate peace with the Allies, as well as for democracy, universal suffrage and meaningful land reform in Hungary. The program also acknowledged the "right of self-determination" of the non-Magyar peoples of Hungary. Within a four-day period, October 27–30, the Romanians of Bukovina, the Ukrainians of Galicia, the Czechs and the Slovaks all announced secession from the empire.

On October 28, police in Budapest fired at demonstrators on the Chain Bridge. The protesters were demanding the appointment of the reformer Count Karolyi as the new Hungarian premier. Rather than bow to reform, the defiant emperor picked Count Janos Hadik—a favorite of the landed elite—to lead the government. But the Hadik government had no effective control of the streets of the capital, where the residents were on the verge of revolution.

Units of the Territorial Army, which had pledged their support of the Hungarian National Council, seized Budapest railroad stations, the central telephone exchange and key government buildings on the night of October 30. Hadik resigned the following day, and the alarmed emperor named Count Karolyi premier. Karolyi quickly created a center-left government that promised policies based on the Hungarian National Council's 12-point plan. Among other things, the plan called for universal sufferage, land reform and much-improved conditions for workers in the cities.

World War I ended for Austria-Hungary on November 3, 1918, when the empire signed an armistice with the Allies in Padua, Italy. The old Hapsburg regime had attempted to regain past glory by going to war. As it turn out, the war destroyed their empire.

Postwar Struggles

Emperor Charles I announced on November 11, 1918 that he would no longer take "any part in the affairs of government." He then moved to Switzerland as a private citizen. The Austrian parliament regarded the statement as an abdication of the throne, and the lawmakers proclaimed Austria a republic on November 12. The Dual Monarchy officially ended on November 16, 1918, when the Karolyi government proclaimed Hungary a republic. The proclamation marked the beginning of Hungary as a modern, independent country.

Karolyi quickly learned that proclaiming a republic, and maintaining a strong, viable government were two very different things. Although he was a capable politician and administrator, the new premier was by nature a centrist who relied on the consensus of diverse political elements in his decisions. Getting a consensus to deal with the overwhelming problems of the postwar period was nearly impossible.

First of all, Hungary's economy was in a shambles. The dissolution of the Dual Monarchy destroyed the integrated financial system that Austria and Hungary had shared for more than 50 years. Secondly, the Allies had imposed economic sanctions on Hungary that were to remain until the matter of war reparations was settled.

French troops occupied much of eastern Hungary and parts of the Slavic lands that had been under Hungarian and Austrian rule. The French did not object when, in the period between October 1918 and January 1919, the formerly subjugated nationalities seized Hungarian property in those lands. Romania in January 1919 annexed all of Transylvania, with no opposition from the French occupation forces in that region.

Even though the Karolyi government professed support for "self-determination," it was stunned by the land seizures and embittered by the Allies' indifference. The Allies were of a mind to punish Austria-Hungary for siding with Germany in the war, so Karolyi's appeals to preserve Hungarian territorial integrity received little sympathy. Inside Hungary, political elements of the far left and far right tugged, pushed and prodded the government toward extreme actions.

The far left—Communists and radical Socialists—had been influenced by Russia's Bolshevik Revolution of 1917. Some had been prisoners of war in Russia during the revolution and returned to Hungary inspired by Marxist-Leninist ideals. Others were Hungarians who actually had fought on the side of the Bolsheviks in Russia, and who were determined to lead a similar revolution in Hungary. One such man was Bela Kun, who considered himself a protege of V. I. Lenin, the father of Soviet Communism. Kun founded the Hungarian Communist Party in Budapest in November 1918.

Communism, as defined by German social theorists Karl Marx and Friedrich Engels, would create an ideal society in which all means of production (as well as political power) would be in the hands of the workers. Marx and Engels regarded capitalism as a necessary interim phase between feudalism and communism. Lenin took their theory a step further. He believed only through revolution, not evolution, could capitalism be overcome and communism implemented.

While the far left openly organized industrial workers, miners and peasant farmers, the far right—mainly current and former army officers—established secret paramilitary groups. The most prominent figure of the extreme right was Gyula Gombos de Jafka, an aide on the Hungarian general staff who attempted to unite the paramilitary groups under his own organization, the National Militia Association.

The Hungarian parliament and the Karolyi government swiftly instituted major reforms in 1918. Laws were passed guaranteeing freedom of the press, freedom of speech and freedom of assembly. Any person over 21 who had been a Hungarian citizen for at least six years was granted the right to vote, and elections were to be held by secret ballot. The new laws were popular with everyone except the elite landowners, who feared their power would be eroded by popular democracy.

Early in 1919, while parliament wrestled with land reform, Hungary was swept with a series of crippling industrial strikes that were instigated by the Communists. Karolyi stepped down as premier and was replaced by a former justice minister, Denes Berinkey, and the leftist Social Democrats took a more visible role in the ruling coalition. (The Social Democrats asserted that they, not the Communists, were the true representatives of the working class.) Karolyi became the republic's first president in January 1919.

Parliament passed a law giving the police power to jail anyone suspected of being an enemy of the state. But rather than being used against the Communists, the law was used to jail right-wingers in the army, whom the government believed might pose the threat of an eventual military takeover. The authorities banned Gombos' National Militia Association.

On February 6, 1919, parliament finally passed a land-reform law. (Land reform had been discussed in political circles, but not implemented, over the course of more than 70 years.) Under the statute, all estates of at least 741 acres were subject to expropriation by the government, with the land being distributed in parcels to small- and dwarf-holding peasant farmers. (Dwarfholders were farmers who owned less than 7 acres of land.) The owners of the expropriated lands, however, were to be compensated in part by taxes on those who received the parcels. If the taxes were not paid, the land was returned to its original owner.

The law satisfied no one. The big landowners opposed the legislation. Smallholders and dwarfholders complained that they could not possibly meet the tax burden. Landless peasants, who made up 96 percent of the peasant class, were to receive nothing at all. Poor farmers, with the urging of the Communists, began seizing estates outright soon after the law was passed. Communist-controlled "peasants' committees" took over several rural county governments.

In response to this, the government jailed approximately 50 Communist leaders—Kun was not among them—on February 21. That did not halt their activities; not only did the leaders continue to give orders from their prison cells, but they also used the opportunity to radicalize fellow prisoners. Communist agitators on the outside gathered strength for a mass protest to free their leaders by force.

It appeared that widespread political violence was on the horizon. President Karolyi took a gamble that he hoped would bring some peace and stability: he attempted to quiet the far left, while at the same time undercutting the Communists, by having the Social Democrats lead a new government. But the Social Democrats realized that they would have no credibility with the masses unless the Communists also had a major political role. The two parties combined to form one ruling body, the Revolutionary Governing Council, on March 21. The chairman of the council—a rank equivalent to premier—was a moderate Social Democrat named Sandor Garbai. But the person really in charge was Communist Party boss Bela Kun, who modestly took the post of foreign minister.

The first official act of the Revolutionary Ruling Council came on March 22, 1919. It abolished parliament, announced its intent to form a "dictatorship of the proletariat" (working class), and proclaimed a Hungarian Soviet Republic. Hungary thus became the first nation in history outside of Soviet Russia with a Communist government.

Red Terror/White Terror

Between March 25 and March 30, 1919, the Revolutionary Ruling Council issued a series of decrees aimed at a radical transformation of Hungarian society. The council nationalized all banks, insurance companies, mines and transportation systems. It handed over factories to "workers' councils." It placed all private and church schools under state control. (The Roman Catholic Church owned more than 60 percent of Hungary's elementary and middle schools.) It abolished the regular court system and replaced it with "workers' tribunals." The council also reorganized the army as a pro-Communist Hungarian Red Army, and created the Hungarian Red Guard, a Communist-controlled militia charged with maintaining internal order.

On April 3, the council took its biggest step: it abolished all private property and decreed a massive land-reform program. All middle-sized and large estates were expropriated by the state with no compensation for the owners. However, the program contained an important catch: the peasants would not receive any private plots. Instead, the estates were transformed into collective farms.

There was no strong opposition to these decrees. Centrist and right-wing politicians either fled the capital (or the country), or were cowed into silence by the Red Guard. The church and big landowners complained, but were politically powerless to stop their property from being seized. Landless peasants resented the fact that they still were not going to receive any land of their own, but soldiers and militia kept them quiet. On the other hand, tens of thousands of industrial workers applauded the changes.

Outside Hungary, the Allied countries were alarmed. At the time the council took power, the United States, Britain, France and other countries were attempting to militarily overthrow the Communists in Russia. Now, suddenly, there was a Marxist-Leninist state in Central Europe. They feared that Hungary might attempt to spread communism to Austria, or even Germany. Soviet Russia was the only country to give Hungary's new government diplomatic recognition.

Romania, apparently with the quiet approval of France, invaded southeast Hungary in mid-April in order to secure its hold on Transylvania. When Hungarian troops failed to halt the onslaught, Romanian forces pushed all the way to the Tisza River, in eastern Hungary. In May, a frightened Revolutionary Ruling Council directed units of the Red Army into Slovakia and Ruthenia so as to open a corridor between Hungary and Russia. The council hoped that Russia would send troops to help Hungary battle against Romania, but the Lenin regime was too preoccupied with the Allied military intervention in Russia to offer any such aid. The Hungarian Red Army was fought to a standstill in Slovakia by troops of the newly formed Czech army. On June 3, 1919, Hungarian opposition figures formed a coalition rival government in the southeastern Hungarian city of Szeged, which the Communists had abandoned before the Romanian invasion. Count Karolyi, who had once been Hungary's president, assumed leadership of the rival government. Count Pal Teleki, a political moderate, was the foreign minister. Admiral Miklos Horthy de Nagybanya—a former military aide to Emperor Francis Joseph—led the so-called National Army, a force recruited by right-wing activist Gyula Gombos de Jafka.

As June progressed, both domestic and foreign situations deteriorated rapidly for the Revolutionary Ruling Council. The inability to defeat the Czechs in Slovakia and the Romanians in eastern Hungary discredited the Red Army. Shortages of fuel and food made the population restless. Communism lost favor in the countryside because landless peasants refused to accept collectivization. As public disorders mounted, the council used the police and Red Guard to crack down on the public. The crackdown, which included arbitrary jailings and torture, became known as the "Red Terror."

By the end of July, Romanian troops had crossed the Tisza and were approaching Budapest. The Allies proposed to intercede with the Romanians— to prevent a takeover of most of Hungary by Romania—but only

The Hungarian regent, Admiral Miklos Horthy (far right), confers with visiting German, Italian and Austrian officers during 1937 military maneuvers in Hungary. (Wide World Photos)

if the Revolutionary Ruling Council stepped down. The council initially resisted the proposal, but gave in when the Social Democrats (who resented the Communist domination of the council) withdrew from the ruling coalition. The council formally resigned on August 1, 1919 and its leaders quickly left the country. The Hungarian Soviet Republic was no more. Romanian troops entered Budapest on August 3, 1919 with no resistance and remained in Hungary until October 1919.

Hungary endured nearly a year of political instability and social chaos following the end of the Communist reign. The period became known as the era of "White Terror." The term "white" signified anticommunist. As many as 5,000 people were killed during the White Terror, and tens of thousands were imprisoned without trial. Known or suspected Communists and radical Socialists, as well as Jews —who were identified with communism in the public mind—were hunted down and jailed by the authorities or murdered by right-wing vigilante groups.

Taken together, the two periods of terror—the Red Terror and the White Terror—revealed to Hungarians a vicious social undercurrent that they had never experienced in modern times. It would surface decades later in the form of the fascism during World War II, and after that in the guise of the Communist secret police.

The most significant political event prior to the summer of 1920 was the appointment by parliament of Admiral Miklos Horthy to the post of regent. (A regent is someone, not necessarily of royal blood, who rules in place of a monarch.) Horthy had returned to Budapest on November 16, 1919 at the head of the 25,000-man National Army, the fighting force of the Szeged opposition government.

Horthy assumed the regency after a lengthy debate in parliament over the future of Hungary's King Charles IV (the former Emperor Charles I), the last of Austria's Hapsburg rulers. Charles had been living in Switzerland since renouncing the throne of Austria-Hungary in 1918. Since he had never formally abdicated as king of Hungary, some members of parliament—backed by wealthy landowners and the Roman Catholic Church—supported his return. Others argued that Hungary should only have an elected, figurehead king, if any king at all. The Horthy regency was the result of a compromise.

From August 1919 to July 1920, Hungary was ruled by a series of interim governments. National elections were held in January 1920 and the new National Smallholders' Party, which mainly represented middle-class landowners, won 40 percent of the seats in the newly restored National Assembly (parliament). Smallholder Sandor Simonyi-Semadam became the premier in March 1920.

Together, these different governments repealed nearly all the decrees of the Revolutionary Ruling Council. Private property was again legal and land reform was rolled back. The elite landowners got back their estates, but their political power was in decline. The governments not only failed to improve Hungary's ruined economy, but they were also unable to keep Hungary's territories from being snatched away by the victorious Allied powers.

The Treaty of Trianon

The victorious Allies, known as the "Great Powers" after World War I, and the defeated Central Powers began peace talks in Paris in April 1919 over such issues as war reparations and the disposition of territories. The Great

Powers did not accept Hungary's argument that it had been only a reluctant partner of Germany and had not sought any territorial gains in the war. The victors, particularly France, were in a punitive mood, and the result was the Treaty of Trianon.

The treaty, signed on June 4, 1920, dismembered what had been the prewar Kingdom of Hungary. The terms outraged Magyars and inspired a popular slogan of resistance: "No, no, never!" To this day, many Hungarians resent what was imposed on them in Paris in 1920. The treaty wounded Hungary's national pride. To the average Hungarian in 1920, the neighboring Slav lands were as much a part of Hungary as the city of Budapest or the Great Plain. It was inconceivable to most Hungarians that those lands could be taken away by the stroke of a pen. The Allies and the Slavs, of course, had a much different view. They regarded the Magyars as persecutors and tyrants. The treaty was the price Hungary had to pay to end the Allied economic boycott of Hungary and to reenter the world community of nations.

In essence, the treaty forced Hungary to relinquish 89,748 square miles of territory and 13.3 million people. Prewar Hungary had comprised 125,641 square miles and a total population of 20.9 million. The treaty reduced Hungary to an area of 35,983 square miles and a population (according to a 1920 census) of 7.6 million. The treaty awarded all of Transylvania, plus two small neighboring regions, to Romania. That amounted to 31.6 percent of Hungary's prewar land and 5.3 million people. The new nation of Czechoslovakia (which incorporated Slovakia and Ruthenia) received 19.34 percent of Hungary's prewar lands and 3.3 million people. The new Kingdom of Serbs, Croats and Slovenes (which would be renamed Yugoslavia in 1929) received 6.4 percent of prewar Hungarian territory and 1.5 million people.

A major concern of Hungary was that the treaty left 3.3 million Magyars living in areas that were now under Romanian or Slavic control. That figure included 1.7 million Magyars in Romania (mainly in Transylvania), 1 million in Czechoslovakia (mainly in Slovakia), and more than 500,000 in the soon-to-be Yugoslavia (mainly in northern Serbia). About 350,000 Magyars emigrated to Hungary from the ceded territories soon after the treaty was signed. With its economy wrecked, Hungary could barely absorb the immigrants.

In addition to the Treaty of Trianon stripping Hungary of its subject territories, the document also prohibited Hungary from having a standing army of more than 35,000 men—with no tanks or heavy artillery. So, Hungary entered the postwar period with vastly shrunken borders, a devastated economy and no military to speak of. The stage was set for the Horthy Era.

The Horthy Era Begins

The authoritarian Horthy Era—the period of the regency of Admiral Miklos Horthy de Nagybanya—which began in 1920 and peaked in 1930, was one of the most stable periods in Hungarian history. But it also laid the groundwork for Hungary's slide toward fascism and its disastrous alliance with Nazi Germany in World War II. It was because of that alliance that Hungary ended up a satellite of the Soviet Union from the late 1940s until the early 1990s.

In July 1920, when Count Pal Teleki took over as premier, the economy was in a shambles. One-half of the nation's work force, including 150,000 workers in Budapest alone, were unemployed. Inflation (uncontrolled price rises) was running at about 6,000 percent, meaning the national currency, the crown, was worth 1/6,000th of its prewar value. Crop yields were a fraction of what they had been before the war.

The Teleki government was unsuccessful in easing the country's economic plight, but it did institute a modest land-reform program. Under the program, the owners of large estates voluntarily distributed 1.1 million acres of land to about 100,000 landless peasants and 300,000 smallholders. The program left more than 19 million acres in the hands of the rich, however.

Teleki resigned as premier in April 1920 and was succeeded by the government leader who was to be most closely associated with the Horthy Era, Count Istvan Bethlen. Bethlen had a talent for gaining the respect of many political and social factions. The landed gentry respected him because he was from a wealthy landowning family. The right wing respected him because, in 1919, he had organized a group of Hungarian exiles in Vienna to oppose the Hungarian Communist regime. The center-left, most particularly the reformed Social Democrats, respected him because of his vigorous efforts to free jailed leftists and halt the remnants of the "White Terror."

The new premier was faced with a crisis in October 1920, when King Charles IV came back to Hungary from Switzerland with the support of some army units that wanted him to return to the throne. Premier Bethlen and Admiral Horthy rallied a force of army troops and right-wing militiamen (led by Gyula Gombos) to defeat the king's forces in a battle west of Budapest on October 23. Horthy captured King Charles and later exiled him to an island off the coast of Portugal. Charles, the last monarch to wear the Crown of St. Stephen, died in exile in 1922.

Bethlen's power base was the Christian Social Party (renamed the Unity Party in 1922), which he forged into a broad-based alliance of wealthy landowners, impoverished gentry (those who had owned land in the Slavic territories taken away from Hungary), the urban Christian middle class, government bureaucrats, and, for a time, extreme-right civilian and

Hungarian peasant farmers in 1935. (Wide World Photos)

military figures. The far-right faction, led by Gombos, broke away from the party in 1923 and formed its own political organization, the Party of Racial Defense. Gombos later returned to the Unity Party and became one of its most powerful figures.

Even with a degree of political stability, the country's economic recovery was slow. The government attempted to counter rampant inflation—16,300 percent in 1924— with wage and price controls. The government banned businesses from raising their prices or increasing their workers' pay. The controls inevitably led to shortages and a decline in the standard of living, particularly in the rural areas. Industrial production continued to lag; it was only 60 percent of prewar levels in 1924. High tariffs (taxes on imports) in the other countries of Europe made it more difficult for Hungary to export goods.

Hungary joined the League of Nations (a forerunner to the United Nations) in 1923, and in 1924, was able to get a loan from the league of 250 million gold crowns at an annual interest rate of 7.5 percent. The loan was conditioned on Hungary honoring the terms of the Treaty of Trianon. The loan was crucial because the Hungarian national treasury was empty and no international banks or individual countries were willing to lend Hungary money to aid its economic recovery. Bethlen used the loan to help stabilize Hungary's currency and subsidize exports. In 1927, the government replaced the crown with a new currency, the pengo, to fight inflation. One pengo was equal to 1,250 paper crowns.

Hungary became increasingly protectionist. It placed high tariffs on imported goods in the late 1920s, thus shielding domestic industries from foreign competition. With the aid of foreign capital investment and more foreign loans, unemployment dropped to about 15 percent and overall production picked up.

But the recovery was painfully slow, and Hungarian workers were angry. A series of strikes instigated by the far left failed to dampen the recovery. The Communist Party had been banned in 1921, but underground Communists and other radicals joined united to form the Socialist Workers' Party in 1925. The party had little support on the national level, but it began to attract some dissatisfied laborers in the major cities in Hungary.

Bethlen's only real political challenge came from the so-called Democratic Bloc, a center-left coalition of the Social Democrats and the new National Bourgeois-Democratic Party (a forerunner of the current Alliance of Free Democrats). The bloc drew support from Jews, moderate leftist intellectuals and people who wanted Hungary to be ruled as a constitutional monarchy. The bloc demanded labor reforms, more land reform, and an end to the government's anti-Semitic policies. (Right-wingers blamed Jews for Hungary's economic problems. Official anti-Semitism was on the rise and would greatly increase in the late 1930s, when Hungary was aligning itself with Nazi Germany. Jews would be banned from government work and universities, and prohibited from owning real estate and certain businesses.)

Bethlen outflanked the opposition by issuing a decree in 1926 to re-create an upper house of parliament that would be filled by hereditary members of the aristocracy. These members would be appointed by the regent. Since the aristocracy supported the ruling Unity Party, the government could effectively block any opposition legislation. In the parliamentary elections of December 1926, the Unity Party captured 60 percent of the vote and 170 seats, solidifying the government's hold.

Hungary dutifully adhered to the Treaty of Trianon throughout the 1920s, although the document inspired simmering resentment among the proud Magyars over the lost Slavic lands. However, the country was too weak militarily to recover by force the territorities that were taken away, and the flow of foreign loans, upon which Hungary's economic recovery depended, would cease if Hungary violated the treaty.

The closest Hungary came to breaking the treaty was in 1925, when it was revealed that the government had counterfeited French and Czechoslovakian bank notes in order to finance Magyar opposition activities in Slovakia. (Bethlen and former Premier Pal Teleki were apparently behind the forgery operation.) France was angered, and Czechoslovakia briefly threatened to invade Hungary. But the scandal was played down by the other Great Powers on the ground that no real harm had been done.

Flirting with Fascism

The Great Depression hit Hungary in 1931, reversing the country's modest economic recovery of the 1920s. The depression was a worldwide economic downturn triggered by the collapse of the U.S. stock market in October 1929. It was characterized by massive unemployment, bank failures, business shutdowns and falling agricultural prices. The economic upheaval drove many Hungarians into movements of the extreme right, which promised better times to come.

The depression shattered Hungary. Almost overnight, 15 percent of the country's factories shut down and 30 percent of the industrial labor force was unemployed. Those who retained their jobs in the government and private sectors were forced to accept drastic pay cuts. Agriculture industry was crippled by declining prices and mounting surpluses. More than 60,000 small and medium-sized farms were abandoned when their owners defaulted on bank loans. Nearly 500,000 farm laborers could not find work. The country's biggest bank, the Hungarian General Credit Bank, narrowly averted bankruptcy.

To make matters worse, Hungary's foreign debt stood at $1 billion (in 1930 U.S. dollars), at that time an astronomical sum for such a small country. The foreign credit that had fueled the economic recovery now was a weight around the nation's neck. Unrest spread throughout Hungary. Unemployed workers and jobless farm laborers rioted, triggering harsh responses by the police. And nearly a decade of political stability crumbled.

Two key factions of the ruling Unity Party—wealthy landowners and middle-class farmers—left to form their own political organization, the Independent Smallholders' Party. One of the founders, Zoltan Tildy, would play a major role in the post World War II era. The Unity Party narrowly won the parliamentary elections of June 1931, but Premier Bethlen resigned two months later. Admiral Horthy named Count Gyula Karolyi to the post.

The Karolyi government was unable to ease the impact of the depression, and he personally was unable to mediate among quarreling factions in the Unity Party. As a result, Horthy fired Karolyi in September 1932 and appointed the popular war minister, Gyula Gombos de Jafka, premier.

Gombos was the most visible of Hungary's right-wing nationalists. He was an open admirer of such Fascist leaders as Benito Mussolini, who had come to power in Italy in 1922, and Adolf Hitler, who came to power in Germany in 1933. He favored an alliance of Hungary with the two great Fascist powers.

Under fascism, all the key elements of society—political, economic and military—unite, usually under a dictatorial leader, to achieve a national purpose set by the leader.

Nationalism is a strong, sometimes obsessive, devotion by a people to their own interests. According to historian Hans Kohn, nationalism goes beyond simple pride in one's culture or traditions. Nationalism is, he says:

The conviction of being a people chosen by God or History has, in ancient and again in modern times, sometimes even fused with a biological belief in the value of common descent and racial purity, in the embodiment of the true faith or the true civilization in people of one "seed" or "blood."[1]

Taken to an extreme, Kohn argues, nationalism results in the belief that only your own ethnic group should rule, and that people outside of your group should be ruled. In other words:

Fascism [is] an exaggerated, self-centered form of nationalism.[2]

Gombos' political good fortune inspired the founding in the 1930s of a host of Hungarian Fascist parties and organizations. They included the National Socialist Hungarian Workers' Party (later renamed the Scythe Cross Movement), the United National Socialist Party, the Party of National Will and the Racial Defense Socialist Party.

Although differing slightly in agendas, all of these Fascist groups were virulently anti-Semitic (while espousing "Christian values") and anti-foreigner (while emphasizing Magyar "racial" and cultural superiority). They opposed Hungary's traditional aristocracy and exalted the working classes. They disparaged "bourgeois [middle-class] democracy" as practiced in the United States, Great Britain and France. And they called for a return of Hungary's "stolen lands," using hatred of the Treaty of Trianon as a tool to recruit followers.

In spite of Gombos' popularity, Hungary never became a true Fascist state, except for a brief period in 1944–45. There were other prominent leaders of the extreme right—Ferenc Szalasi, Count Fidel Palffy and Zoltan Boszormeny—and they were each too personally ambitious to unite under Gombos. Also, Hungary's aristocrats and leftists in the 1930s still posed a formidable political opposition.

But the most significant factor contributing to Hungary's failure to become a Fascist state in the 1930s was Gombos' sudden death—apparently of natural causes—in October 1935, while on a visit to the Nazi German capital of Berlin. A few months before he died, the Unity Party won a narrow victory in parliamentary elections that were tainted with widespread vote-rigging.

During his three years as premier, Gombos had succeeded in drawing Hungary closer to Italy and Germany. The Gombos government was able to persuade Germany to open its market to Hungarian produce, and did secure some loans from the German government. However, the premier had a more important motive behind his drive to align Hungary with the Fascist powers: he wanted Hitler and Mussolini to use their influence to help Hungary recover its lost territories.

Gombos' successor as premier was Kalman Daranyi, a cautious conservative who was wary of aligning Hungary too closely with Germany, remembering the ill-fated Hungarian-German alliance in the First World War. Under Daranyi, there was a modest crackdown on the extreme right, which he regarded as a threat to the status quo. One of those sent to jail in 1938 was Ferenc Szalasi, who had become Hungary's most prominent Fascist since the death of Gombos.

Szalasi was the creator of "Hungarianism," a philosophy that incorporated Magyar nationalism with German National-Socialist (Nazi) principles. Szalasi founded the Party of National Will in 1937, but it was banned by the government. In 1939, while he was in prison, his followers founded the Arrow Cross Party/Hungarist Movement, a Fascist organization that became one of the two most important far-right groups in Hungary in the late 1930s. The other was the National Socialist Hungarian Party.

The Daranyi government quietly accepted Germany's forced takeover of Austria, in March 1938. The takeover, combined with Hitler's open designs on Czechoslovakia, scared all but the most right-wing Hungarians. Daranyi redirected government spending toward rearmament, and ordered a buildup of Hungary's army far beyond the 35,000-man limit set by the Treaty of Trianon. The Great Powers did not care about this treaty violation because they were too preoccupied with Germany's activities.

Admiral Horthy dismissed Daranyi in May 1938 and appointed as premier Bela Imredy, the head of the National Bank. Imredy attempted to steer a neutral course by balancing Hungary's ties to Germany and Italy with closer Hungarian ties to Great Britain and Poland.

The Munich Agreement of September 1938 forced Czechoslovakia to cede its Sudentenland region to Germany. Hitler then made it clear to the Imredy government that if Hungary wanted German help in recovering its lost lands, then it would have to actively support any further German moves against Czechoslovakia. Germany would absorb most of Czechoslovakia in mid-March 1939, with no objection from Hungary.

Following the Munich Agreement, Hungary held talks with Czechoslo-vakia over a "voluntary" return of Hungarian territories. German foreign minister Joachim von Ribbentrop and Italian foreign minister Galeazzo Ciano acted as mediators. On November 2, 1938, at a conference in Vienna, Ribbentrop and Ciano ruled that Hungary was the rightful owner of 4,615 square miles of the eastern Czechoslovak regions of Slovakia and Carpatho-Ukraine (formerly Ruthenia). The effected areas contained 1.1 million people, including 590,000 Magyars.

At first, the Hungarian public rejoiced at the return of land and the repatriation of the Magyars. But the mood soured into complaints that the ruling, known as the Vienna Award, only encompassed a relatively narrow strip along Hungary's border with Czechoslovakia. Imredy had hoped for, and did not receive, a common border with Poland, which was north of a point where Slovakia touched Carpatho-Ukraine in an area not included in the Vienna Award. When Hungary made preparations to take the remainder of Carpatho-Ukraine by force, Hitler adamantly forbade the move.

Imredy resigned on November 23, 1938, but again accepted the premier's post when Horthy was unable to find anyone willing to take the job. Imredy formed a new cabinet, this one with a noticeable right-wing cast. It included as foreign minister Count Istvan Csaky, who made no secret of his admiration for Nazi Germany.

Imredy's second term as head of the government lasted only until February 1939. Horthy dismissed him on the pretext of discovering Jewish ancestry in Imredy's family. Count Pal Teleki, a former premier, once again headed the government. But Foreign Minister Csaky and other right-wingers remained in the cabinet and wielded great influence.

Teleki, bending to cabinet pressure, forged closer Hungarian-German relations. Hungary received its reward in March 1939, when Germany did not interfere with Hungary's seizure of the entire Carpatho-Ukraine. A month later, Hungary occupied an adjacent chunk of Slovakia, thus attaining its coveted common border with Poland. Together, the seizures gave Hungary an additional 4,800 square miles of territory and more than 500,000 people, a majority of whom were ethnic Ukrainians.

Recovering portions of the lost lands boosted the credibility of the right wing among the Hungarian populace. Teleki's own center-right organiza-tion, the Party of Hungarian Life, won 181 of 260 contested seats in the elections of March 1939. Extreme-right parties captured 48 seats, making them the second-strongest political force in parliament.

In the Axis

Germany invaded Poland on September 1, 1939, beginning World War II, the bloodiest conflict in history. By 1945, at the end of the war, over 50 million people were dead and property damage was in the trillions of dollars. The issues surrounding the war were simpler and more straightforward than those in World War I. The Allied nations successfully defeated an attempt by the Axis powers to achieve worldwide military domination. The major Allies were the U.S., Great Britain, the Soviet Union, China, France and Canada. The main Axis countries were Germany, Japan and Italy.

Hungary, Romania and Bulgaria were among the less powerful Axis partners. Hungary did not formally join the Axis alliance until a year after the war began. It would deeply regret its involvement.

In the beginning, Hungary wanted no part of the war. Premier Teleki quickly declared Hungry a "nonbelligerent" nation following the German invasion of Poland. In addition—as if to show its independence from the Nazis—Hungary opened its new border with Poland and granted political asylum to approximately 150,000 fleeing Poles.

Teleki attempted to navigate a very difficult course: Hungary increasingly supplied the German war machine with raw materials (oil, bauxite, iron) and farm goods, while at the same time refusing to commit any troops to the Axis cause. He justified the policy with the explanation that Hungary's friendship with the Fascist powers was based solely on a desire to get back all of its lost territories. He even privately assured the British that Hungary was not completely on the side of the Germans.

Teleki's caution was not popular at home. Many Hungarians were dazzled by the Axis powers' initial military successes, and they wanted Hungary to get some of the bounty, or at least to get back all of the lost lands. With the economy on a war footing, thousands of new jobs opened up and wages rose. The ranks of Hungarian Fascist groups swelled, particularly Ferenc Szalasi's militant Arrow Cross movement.

When in 1940 the Soviet Union bullied Romania into handing over Bessarabia (a region on the Soviet-Romanian border), public pressure impelled Teleki to try the same tactic to force Romania to return Transylvania. Since Romania was a major supplier of oil to Germany, Hitler did not want to risk the disruption of a Hungary-Romania war. As a result,

The Jews of Hungary

The first Jews arrived in Hungary at the invitation of King Stephen in the 12th century. By 1787, Jews numbered 83,000, or 1 percent of Hungary's population. There followed a heavy Jewish immigration, particularly from Galicia (a region in East-Central Europe) and from the Czech land of Moravia. In 1880, there were 700,000 Jews in Hungary.

The Jewish people did not find it difficult to assimilate. They willingly adopted the Magyar language and some aspects of Magyar culture. Laws in 1859 and 1867 gave them full legal protection and civil rights equal to those of other Hungarians. Unlike other countries in Central Europe, few Hungarian Jews lived in rural communities. Most settled in large towns and cities, especially in Budapest, and on large estates.

Jews made up Hungary's first real middle class. They became business owners, bankers, lawyers, doctors and teachers. Jewish capital financed the growth of Hungary's major industries.

After World War I, Hungary's Jews suffered from increasing persecution. First, they were blamed unfairly for the brief Communist dictatorship of Bela Kun. Then, in the 1930s and early 1940s, a succession of pro-Fascist Hungarian governments passed laws that took away their legal protections and civil liberties. Many Jews, such as renowned playwright Ferenc Molnar, chose to leave Hungary.

In 1944, an estimated 450,000 Hungarian Jews were displaced to Nazi German concentration camps, where most perished. Today, about 80,000 Jews remain in Hungary.

Germany and Italy again decided in favor of a Hungarian territorial claim. The Second Vienna Award, made on August 30, 1940, gave Hungary 16,500 square miles of northern Transylvania. The recovered region contained 2.5 million people, mainly Magyar residents.

Teleki continued on a contradictory course. Lured by the prospect of recovering more lost territory, on November 20, 1940, Hungary formally joined the Axis by signing the Tripartite Pact (the alliance of Germany, Italy and Japan). But less than a month later, Hungary signed a friendship pact with Yugoslavia—in spite of the fact that Germany had plans to take over Yugoslavia.

When the Germans invaded Yugoslavia in March 1941, Hitler demanded that his troops be allowed passage through Hungary. Teleki refused, and was vilified, not only by the Hungarian political right, but by the regent, Admiral Horthy. On April 3, a despondent Teleki committed suicide.

The new premier was Laszlo Bardossy, who had replaced Istvan Csaky as foreign minister in February 1941. Bardossy did not like the Nazis, but was convinced Germany was going to win the war. He wanted Hungary to be firmly on the winning side.

Bardossy directed Hungarian forces to follow the German army into Yugoslavia and take over the Bacska region, about 4,200 square miles that had been taken away from Hungary in 1920. With this move, Hungary regained a significant amount of territory—more than 50 percent of its pre-Trianon lands—and got back more than 5 million people, including over 2 million Magyars. The Bardossy government immediately launched the same kind of "Magyarization" program among its recaptured Slavic subjects that had caused so much resentment prior to World War I. Once again, Hungary forced its Slavs to adopt Magyar customs and use the Magyar language.

Hitler would not let Hungary enjoy the rewards of Axis partnership without exacting a price: Hungary's active participation in the war. When Germany invaded the Soviet Union in June 1941, Hungary sent along about 40,000 troops. The Nazi offensive stalled several months later, and the compliant Bardossy acceded to a German demand for many more troops. The Second Hungarian Army, more than 200,000 men, was sent off to fight in the Soviet Union in January 1942.

Bardossy's willingness to commit large numbers of troops to the Russian Front—where the Axis offensive had slowed and casualties were frighteningly high—worried Admiral Horthy. The regent removed Bardossy as premier in March 1942 and named Miklos Kallay, an aristocrat, to the post. Under Kallay, Hungary made no further large-scale commitments of troops to the war, but the country's resources and production continued to be bled by Germany. As Germany was slow in paying for the goods, and stopped paying Hungary altogether in 1943, inflation soared.

Hungarians at home felt the bitter impact of the war in early January 1943, when the Second Hungarian Army was annihilated in a Soviet counterattack near the Russian town of Voronezh. Anti-German sentiment in Hungary rose sharply when it was learned that the army unit had been sacrificed by the Nazis in order to cover retreating German troops. In all, 40,000 men of the Second Army died in the battle. Another 70,000 were taken prisoner by the Soviets, and many of them would die in captivity.

The bloodshed on the Russian Front fueled antiwar sentiment in Hungary. In 1943, Kallay opened secret contacts with the British on the possibility of Hungary withdrawing from the conflict. The sole condition he proposed was that Hungary be allowed to keep its recovered territories when the war ended. But the British insisted that it would not be enough for Hungary to simply stop fighting; Hungary would actually have to declare war on Germany. Kallay's government rejected the idea of Hungary turning against the Axis.

By 1944, Soviet forces were steadily advancing westward toward Hungary, and Hungary was being bombed by the Allies. On March 17, 1944, Hitler ordered Horthy to fire the premier and appoint to the post Lieutenant General Dome Szotjay, a longtime Hungarian ambassador to Germany who was a well-known Nazi sympathizer. Szotjay filled his cabinet with members of the Hungarian National Socialist Alliance, a coalition of Fascist groups.

On March 19, 1944, eight German divisions (about 150,000 troops) moved into Hungary, purportedly at the request of the Szotjay government. With German army and SS (elite guard) units backing him up, Szotjay was free to neutralize all domestic opposition. Thousands of leftists, including leading Social Democrats and Smallholders, and intellectuals and journalists were imprisoned or sent to German concentration camps. The police and Arrow Cross militia rounded up as many as 450,000 Hungarian Jews for deportation to Nazi death camps, a move protested by Horthy and by the Catholic Church.

Up to 20,000 Hungarian Jews escaped deportation thanks to a courageous Swedish diplomant, Raoul Wallenberg. He gave Swedish identity papers that allowed them to leave Hungary under the diplomatic protection of his country. Sweden was officially neutral in the war. Therefore, persons carrying Swedish identity papers were not regarded as combatants. Wallenberg disappeared at the end of the war. He is believed to have been arrested by the Soviets and to have died in a Soviet prison.

The government banned all political parties in August 1944. Horthy gathered the courage to dismiss Szotjay on August 24, and replaced him with a trusted aide, General Geza Lakatos. In September, when Soviet troops crossed the border into Hungary, Lakatos entered secret talks with them over an armistice. Like the British in 1943, the Soviets demanded that Hungary join the fight against Germany. Lakatos reluctantly agreed.

Horthy, with no prior consultation with the Hungarian military, made a nationwide radio broadcast on October 15, 1944. He ordered Hungarian soldiers to stop fighting the Soviets, but he did not order them to turn against the Germans. The reaction was immediate: Arrow Cross militiamen took over government buildings, and German troops seized the Buda Palace (the regent's official residence) and arrested Horthy. SS commandos kidnapped Horthy's youngest son and took him to Germany as a hostage. The Hungarian military High Command reaffirmed its loyalty to it Axis partner.

The Germans threatened to kill Horthy's son, and coerced the former regent into withdrawing his announcement. They also forced Horthy to name Ferenc Szalasi—the head of the Arrow Cross—as Hungary's new head of government. Szalasi, using Hitler as role model, gave himself the title of "leader of the nation." The Nazis kept Horthy under house arrest in the palace. The Horthy Era, which began in 1920, was finished.

For the next four months, the SS and Arrow Cross murdered thousands of people in a reign of terror. As noted by Hungarian historian Joerg K. Hoensch:

> This terror was directed against the new government's political opponents and Jews who had not yet been deported. During the winter of 1944–45, over 80,000 Jews, mainly older people and children, were driven into concentration camps and perished . . . Most of Hungary's provincial Jews fell victim to the extermination measures carried out by the Germans and the Arrow Cross.[3]

During the reign of terror, the Hungarian army collapsed, with thousands of soldiers either surrendering to the Soviets or deserting their units. German forces could not hold back the Soviet offensive. The Germans were forced to pull back to the Buda Hills, across the Danube River, when the Soviet Red Army captured the Pest section of the capital in January 1945. One elderly Hungarian interviewed in 1987 recalled:

> "The Germans defended Buda until the middle of February. They had set up a hospital in the caverns under the castle. As the Nazi troops

prepared to retreat, they killed their own men who were too badly wounded to walk, killed them with flamethrowers, instead of surrendering them to the Russians."[4]

The Soviets captured Buda Castle (freeing Horthy) on February 13, 1945, after heavy fighting that destroyed much of the city and killed many civilians. The last German troops exited Hungary in early April 1945. The remnants of Szalasi's Fascist regime fled with them.

The toll of the conflict was horrendous. No one knows how many Hungarians (including Hungarian Jews sent to Nazi death camps) perished in the conflict, but the figure definitely is in the hundreds of thousands. The capital of Budapest—already heavily damaged by Allied bombings in 1944—was largely destroyed in the street fighting in 1945. Hungary's economic structure was wrecked. And the conflict opened the door to a political takeover by the Communists and four decades of subjugation by the Soviets.

NOTES

1. Hans Kohn, *The Age of Nationalism* (New York: Harper & Brothers, 1962), p. 17.
2. Ibid., p. 26.
3. Joerg K. Hoensch, *A History of Modern Hungary: 1867–1986* (New York: Longman, Inc., 1988), p. 157.
4. Hans Magnus Enzensberger, *Europe, Europe: Forays into a Continent* (New York: Random House, Inc., 1989), p. 129.

3

Hungary Under Communism

The Rise of Communism

At the end of World War II, Hungary faced an uncertain future. Hundreds of thousands of its people had died in the conflict. Transylvania, Carpatho-Ukraine and the other neighboring territories restored to Hungary in 1938–40 were once again lost. The economy was in ruins. Inflation made the national currency, the pengo, worthless. All of the bridges over Hungary's two main rivers, the Danube and the Tisza, had been destroyed. The fighting had demolished one-half of all of the nation's industrial plants. One-half of Hungary's farm livestock was gone. And one out of every four houses in the country had been damaged in the war.

Worse still, the country was occupied by the Soviet Red Army, which had looted and raped its way across Hungary in the last stage of the war. In the name of "reparations," the Soviets had dismantled and shipped back to the U.S.S.R. much of Hungary's undamaged factory equipment. In addition, the Soviets deported more than 250,000 Hungarians to labor camps in Russia's cold, desolate Siberia region. Many of the deportees—soldiers, accused Fascists and anticommunist activists—would not survive the freezing temperatures, back-breaking work and filthy conditions in the labor camps. Most of those who survived the ordeal returned to Hungary broken in mind, body and spirit.

Although a majority of Hungarians did not realize it, their proud little country was about to become an integral part of the Soviet sphere of influence in Eastern Europe. Hungary was destined to become a Soviet satellite, just like Poland, Romania, Czechoslovakia and its neighbors.

With the departure of the Fascists, Hungary was ruled initially by a provisional government of the National Independence Front under General Miklos de Dalnok. The front had been formed in the city of Szeged in December 1944 under the protection of the advancing Soviet Red Army. The organization was a coalition of Hungarian leftist opposition parties: Communists, Social Democrats, National Peasants and Bourgeois-Democrats. The only major opposition party not represented in the front was the Independent Smallholders, led by Zoltan Tildy and Ferenc Nagy. It was the front that signed an armistice with the Allies on January 20, 1945.

The coalition enabled the Communist Party, which had been banned in Hungary since 1921, to emerge into the open. The party was careful to present itself publicly as just another member of the front, but in fact, it was secretly planning to become Hungary's dominant political force. The architect of the plan was Matyas Rakosi, a Hungarian disciple of Soviet leader Joseph Stalin.

Rakosi (1892–1971) had commanded the Red Guard during the short-lived Hungarian Soviet Republic of 1919. He had spent most of the pre–World War II and war years in the U.S.S.R., where he had become a enthusiastic follower of the Stalinist style of communism. Stalinism emphasized rigid obedience to the party and the party leader.

On the orders of the Soviet dictator, Rakosi returned to Hungary in 1945 and took over the leadership of the Hungarian Communist Party from Erno Gero, another Hungarian Marxist who had received his political training in the U.S.S.R.

One aspect of Rakosi's plan called for large numbers of Communists and Communist sympathizers to infiltrate the other parties in the National Independence Front without revealing their true allegiance. Once entrenched in the other parties, they could influence members of those organizations to support policies proposed by the Communist Party. As it turned out, the plan worked very well.

In 1945, the provisional government took two major actions. First, it decreed a large-scale land-reform program. Second, it signed a treaty of friendship and economic cooperation with the Soviet Union.

Under the land-reform decrees of March 1945, the properties held by "Fascists" (real or accused), banks and other financial institutions, as well as much land owned by the Catholic Church, were seized and distributed to the landless peasants, farm laborers and smallholders. The decrees encompassed almost 8 million acres , or nearly 40 percent of Hungary's arable land. More than 600,000 people received parcels of land averaging about 7 acres in size. Some 3.2 million acres of the expropriated lands became the property of the state.

The friendship/economic treaty was signed with the U.S.S.R. in August 1945. The action was protested by the Western democracies, which viewed it as a move by Stalin to bring Hungary under the Soviet wing. The protest died down when the Soviet government agreed to permit free elections in Hungary.

The 1945 Elections

National elections were held in Hungary on November 7, 1945 under the watchful eye of the Allied Control Commission. The commission, which included representatives of the victorious Allied powers, monitored postwar developments in the former Axis nations.

The elections were perhaps the most free ever held in Hungary up to that time. The Independent Smallholders captured 57 percent of the vote and 245 of the 409 seats in the newly revived National Assembly.

The Communist Party, which boasted of having over 600,000 members, won only 70 seats. The Social Democrats finished third, gaining 67 seats.

The surprisingly weak showing of the Communists was attributed to several factors. The party was linked in the public's mind with the Soviets, whose military occupation was widely unpopular. Secondly, the wealthy and middle classes leaned toward the Smallholders, who promised liberal democracy coupled with moderate socialism. The urban working class and trade unions resurrected their prewar loyalty to the Social Democrats.

Perhaps the key factor in the Communists' poor showing was the unwillingness of the Hungarian people to replace fascism with the opposite political extreme. They remembered the widespread violence and disorder of the 1919–20 era, when the "Red Terror" of the far left

A Hungarian collective farm in 1959. Farmers were forced to use oxen due to a shortage of tractors. (Wide World Photos)

had been countered by the "White Terror" of the far right (see p. 28). Voters in 1945 endorsed social change without radicalism.

Zoltan Tildy of the Smallholders became Hungary's first postwar premier. Citing the need for national unity, he created a cabinet that had representatives of all of the major parties. The Communists had only four posts in the cabinet, but two were crucial: Matyas Rakosi was one of the government's two deputy premiers, and Imre Nagy, a Rakosi aide, took over as interior minister.

Nagy (1896–1958) would become the key figure in the anti-Soviet uprising of 1956. He had turned to Marxism while a prisoner of war of the Russians in the First World War. In 1945, Nagy was an enthusiastic Stalinist. He formed the Allam-Vedelmi Osztaly (AVO), or State Security Department, a police organization that would be used eventually to intimidate opponents of the Communists. Illness forced Nagy to give up the post in 1946, but his successor, Laszlo Rajk, was another Rakosi aide.

"Salami Tactics"

Rakosi and the Communists were much more politically astute, and much more treacherous, than their partners in the postwar ruling coalition. Rakosi's intent was simple: to use any means at his disposal to slice away the opposition piece by piece until only the Communists were left in power. He would later characterize the stratagem as "salami tactics."

One of the first cuts of the "salami" came in February 1946, when he convinced Premier Tildy of the need for a Supreme Economic Council to oversee the recovery of the national economy. The council, which was not answerable to the cabinet, had sweeping powers, including the granting of government loans to industry and the distribution of raw materials. Not surprisingly, Communists dominated the council.

At the other end of the spectrum, Communists infiltrated Hungary's trade unions and workers' committees in numbers large enough to sway decision making in those bodies. They also instigated periodic work stoppages, which in turn played into the hands of the Communists in the government, who advocated state control of industries. At the insistence of the Communists, the government took over Hungary's

Imre Nagy in 1956, before the uprising. (Wide World Photos)

ironworks in November 1946, and nationalized all of the country's banks and more than 200 large commercial enterprises a year later.

Meanwhile, Communist-dominated "people's courts" prosecuted more than 40,000 people for war crimes between 1945 and 1948. About 20,000 defendants were convicted and, of those, some 500 were executed. (Among those executed were former Fascist leader Ferenc Szalasi and former premiers Bela Imredy, Laszlo Bardossy and Dome Szotjay.) Although the prosecutions were popular with some Hungarians, they contributed to an atmosphere of fear in the country. Communists in parliament used the fear to increase the government's police powers.

In February 1946, the National Assembly proclaimed a new Republic of Hungary, one that for the first time had no monarch or regent. Premier Tildy became Hungary's first president (head of state). Ferenc Nagy of the Smallholders took over as premier.

The ongoing war-crimes prosecutions inevitably spilled over into the political arena. In early 1947, the Communists claimed to have discovered a right-wing plot to overthrow the government. Several high-ranking figures in the Smallholders' Party were implicated and put on trial. Although their guilt was debatable, it was enough to plant the seeds of discord in the party, which began to splinter with internal bickering. Moderate Smallholders either quit the party or were expelled as it increasingly came under a radical left-wing faction led by Istvan Dobi. Dobi backed an alliance with the Communists.

Ferenc Nagy resigned as premier in May 1947 and was replaced by another Smallholder, Lajos Dinnyes, who was forced to call new elections. By then, the Smallholders were so badly divided into pro- and anticommunist factions they could barely function as a party. The nation's third leading political force, the Social Democratic Party, was filled with Communist sympathizers and therefore provided no real opposition to Communist initiatives. Several small, moderate parties had sprung up in 1946–47, but they were too weak, or too frightened, to provide any real opposition. In the national elections of August 1947, the Communists finished with 100 seats (of 411 contested seats), compared to the Social Democrats' 68 and the Smallholders' 67.

The success of Rakosi's "salami tactics" was now evident. To maintain the illusion that the Communists were not in charge, Rakosi engineered Dinnyes' return as premier. Because he owed his position to the Communists, the premier filled all but four cabinet posts with Communist ministers. That meant that the Rakosi's followers held sway in cabinet votes to determine government policies. Premier Dinnyes was so weak politically that he was compelled to bow to the initiatives of his Communist ministers.

On the foreign scene, Hungary was forced to accept a peace treaty with the Allies that formally returned the country to its 1920 Trianon borders (see p. 40). On February 18, 1948, Hungary joined the Communist Information Bureau (Cominform), a Soviet-led treaty organization supposedly dedicated to the mutual friendship of Communist parties in Eastern Europe. In fact, Cominform was the earliest manifestation of what would be known as the "Eastern Bloc," the U.S.S.R. and its satellites.

Hungary's first president, Zoltan Tildy, resigned in July 1948. The Communist-dominated parliament picked the Communist-leaning Social Democratic leader Arpad Szakasits to succeed Tildy. Tildy wasthe last pro-democracy figure to hold high office in Hungary in the late 1940s.

In December 1948, Smallholder Istvan Dobi—by now an open ally of Rakosi—formed a new government. Communists manned all of the significant cabinet posts. Rakosi was a deputy premier, Laszlo Rajk was the foreign minister, and an up-and-coming young Marxist named Janos Kadar was the interior minister. This would be Hungary's last official non-Communist government until the downfall of communism in 1989.

Stalin's Shadow

In 1948, the Communist Party and the Social Democratic Party merged into a single organization, the Hungarian Workers' Party. Hungary proclaimed itself a "People's Republic." Several governments came and went, but Communists dominated the cabinets. Matyas Rakosi, the Workers' Party boss, was in firm control of the country.

There was no longer any true political opposition in Hungary. By 1949, all of the opposition parties had either disappeared or been consolidated into something called the Independence Popular Front. The front was a Communist-controlled organization, with no real independence or political power, that pretended to be an opposition party. The Communists offered the organization as proof to the West that Hungary still was a democracy.

According to Paul E. Zinner, an American expert on Eastern Europe, Rakosi had a simple and coldblooded concept of how Hungary should be ruled:

> He is said to have expounded his philosophy of government in terms
> of a "law of large numbers." This, he explained, meant "killing some
> [people] and corrupting the rest."[1]

Rakosi took his cues from his idol, Soviet leader Joseph Stalin (1879–1953). In power since 1929, Stalin had gained worldwide admiration for rallying his people to turn back the German-led invasion of the U.S.S.R. in World War II. (An estimated 20 million Soviets died in the war.) However, he was also a ruthless dictator who presided over a brutal police state. Stalin's policies, including the forced collectivization of agriculture (the confiscation of private farms by the government), the mass deportation of ethic minorities to remote areas of the Soviet Union, and the use of secret police and the military to crush dissent, brought suffering to millions of Soviets.

Under Stalin's direction, Soviet-trained Communists like Rakosi gained a foothold and took over the countries of Eastern Europe. Stalin regarded the "satellite" countries as a necessary geographic buffer between the Western democracies and the U.S.S.R. He was determined that if his country ever went to war with the West, the battles would be fought in Eastern Europe, not on Soviet soil. The postwar period of tensions between the Soviet Union and the Western nations, lasting roughly from 1945 to 1990, became known as the Cold War.

Rakosi emulated Stalin in every way. As Stalin had done in the U.S.S.R., Rakosi saw to it that the party had its tentacles in every union hall, every classroom, every factory in Hungary. As described by Zinner, the Communists instituted regimentation and fear in the county:

> . . . Invasion of privacy in a variety of ingenious and highly irritating ways was used to brutalize human sensitivities. Work schedules, compulsory participation in supervised social activities, including [political] seminars and lectures in factories and offices, . . . reduced the amount of leisure time of individuals and the opportunity of families to be together away from the probing scrutiny of their behavior. . . . It was as if the whole working population was under continuous security investigation. Personnel files were kept meticulously to determine the class origin and occupational history of job applicants, and to record entries about their political loyalty and personal demeanor. Called cadre cards (*kader lapok*), . . . they were in fact police files whose very existence put people on guard and impeded social and occupational mobility.[2]

Rakosi's opponents were jailed, executed or simply disappeared. Even his allies were not safe from Stalinist "purges." A purge was a method by which Communist leaders got rid of political rivals or people whose loyalty was in question. Such people were subjected to "show trials," that is, they were prosecuted on false charges, and through torture or threats were made to publicly confess their guilt. Stalin used purges to imprison, exile and execute what some estimate at millions of Soviets in the 1930s. As communism advanced in Eastern Europe after World War II, Rakosi and other Stalinists adopted the purge tactic to instill fear among party and government officials in their own countries. In turn, fearful officials were less likely to challenge or disobey Communist leaders.

Hungary's most infamous show trial was held in 1949. The target, Laszlo Rajk, the Communist former interior minister, was prosecuted for "nationalist deviance," a phrase that encompassed a vague conspiracy against the party. Rajk was made to confess that he had been an "agent of imperialism" since the 1930s. Of course, he was found guilty and executed.

The AVO, the State Security Department, became a more effective tool of terror with the help of advisers from the Soviet NKVD (a forerunner of the KGB secret police). Although the AVO had an undercover arm, the organization was typified by armed thugs in blue uniforms who used threats, beatings and torture to carry out the will of the party.

As if the AVO was not enough, the party created another brutal security organization, the Allam-Vedelmi Hatosag (AVH), or State Security Authority. In addition to keeping watch on ordinary citizens, the AVH kept surveillance on party and government officials to root out disloyalty in high places. As detailed by Hungarian historian Joerg K. Hoensch:

> After 1950, the dynamic Peter Gabor reorganized the various police organizations with the help of Soviet experts. In the new AVH, he developed a perfect technique of fabricating appropriate conspiracies and confessions at the most opportune moment to exploit a political situation. Thanks to its purges, the secret police, which comprised sixteen departments, kept records on over a million citizens and could rely on some 300,000 informers. . . . It became a semi-autonomous institution which eventually only Moscow could control directly. At the same time, the Soviet police kept its own independent secret-police apparatus in Hungary.[3]

Hungary was a police state from the late 1940s through the late 1950s. Hungarians had to be careful of what they said, the places they went and whom they met. Informers were everywhere. Some informers were paid by the secret police to gather information. Others were coerced into informing on coworkers, friends and even family members. Still others felt they had a duty to the country or the party to inform on others.

Hungarians suspected of political crimes—espionage, treason or counter-revolutionary activities—had no legal protections, unlike criminal suspects in the Western democracies. The AVO and AVH could, and did, enter suspects' homes without warrants, and kidnap suspects off the streets. The suspects could be held for questioning as long as the security organizations wanted. Some were tortured until they confessed, even if they had done nothing wrong.

High-ranking religious figures were no more immune to persecution than ordinary Hungarians. When the party placed over 5,000 religious schools under government control, the move was strongly resisted by Jozsef Cardinal Mindszenty, the Roman Catholic primate of Hungary. He was jailed in 1948 as a "subversive," and bravely refused to confess, even when the authorities promised to release him if he would admit guilt. The Vatican (the seat of the Roman Catholic Church) and the Western nations protested Mindszenty's mistreatment, but to no avail.

Economic Failure

Rakosi launched a series of disastrous economic programs in the late 1940s. He attempted to push Hungary, an agrarian country, to rapid Soviet-style "Socialist industrialization." Simply put, Hungary spent millions on the heavy industries, particularly iron and steel production. To pave the way for the program, the government nationalized all companies with 10 or more employees and banned the right to strike.

In rural areas, the government confiscated the lands of the remaining small private farmers and forced thousands of rural families into farm cooperatives and collective farms. Cooperatives were state-owned farms that were run by groups of farmers, who sold their produce to the government. As an incentive, they were allowed to own small parcels of land, from which they could keep some produce for themselves, or even sell it on the private market.

Collectives, or state farms, were run by the government with the farmers as paid employees.

The only resistance to collectivation came from the *kulaks*, or middle-class landowning farmers. The government maintained control by heavily policing the *kulaks*. No one in the rural areas was safe.

> Police interfered in [country dwellers'] lives just as arbitrarily as in the lives of urban dwellers. Flying squads of secret policemen (the dreaded blue-uniformed AVO) swooped down on villages, usually to "aid" with the organization of a collective farm or to "improve" compulsory deliveries of crops. The techniques they employed were simple and effective. Beating or placing a person on a hot stove usually sufficed to soften up resistance to joining a collective or to surrendering hoarded grain.[4]

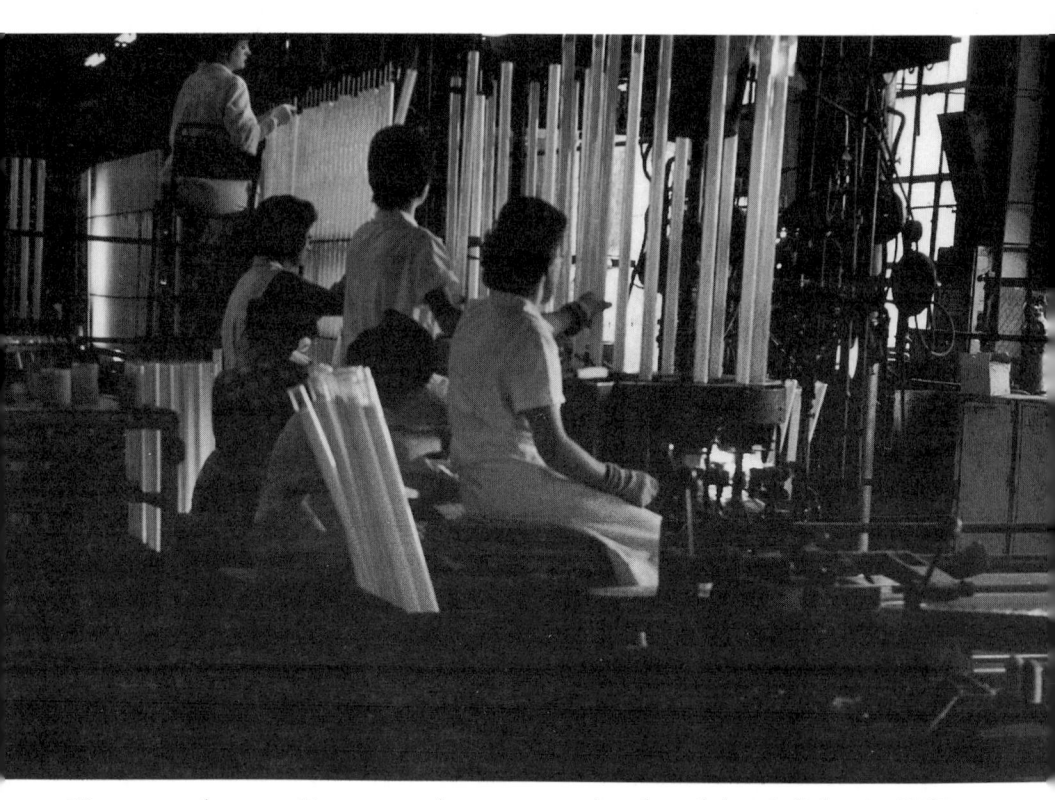

Women employees at Tungsram, the state-owned maker of electric lights, in 1965. Hungary would undertake its "New Economic Mechanism" reforms three years later. (Wide World Photos)

At one point, the Rakosi regime formulated a list of about 38,000 opponents and potential opponents in Budapest. They were all rounded up by the security forces and forced to move into the countryside to work as laborers on collective farms. The government confiscated all their property. The victims of the forced resettlement included 14,000 Jews, over 100 former aristocrats, 85 military generals, plus numerous anticommunist politicians, factory owners, bankers and business executives. The forced exodus had a double benefit from the party's point of view. It got rid of any potential organized opposition in the capital, and it brought much needed labor to the state farms.

Rakosi's economic plans were a complete failure. With 90 percent of all businesses in the hands of the government, economic decisions had to pass through layers of bureaucrats before anything could be accomplished. By 1950, as many as 400,000 Hungarians worked in government offices, an enormous number for so small a country. For example, if the manager of a local steel plant needed some vital new equipment, he was required to submit his request to the central government, where it would be studied by bureaucrats in dozens of departments, and perhaps even be reviewed by party officials. It could take months for the request to be approved or disapproved. Even if it was approved, there was no guarantee the equipment was available.

Also, the industrial production targets had been set much too high, forcing employees into exhausting work schedules. The plants were inefficient and their equipment was in need of modernization. Workers had no incentive to work harder, since their salaries were low and fixed.

Similarly, the only decent farm production was on the few remaining private plots. The families that worked on the cooperative farms rejected the low prices offered by the government. They thought it made better sense to slaughter their livestock and use the money to purchase scarce consumer goods. Farm production actually dropped. Because of this, the government was forced to ration beef and pork.

Hungary's economic woes embarrassed its Soviet masters and lowered Rakosi's stature. When Stalin died in March 1953, his temporary successor, Georgi Malenkov, did not hesitate to humiliate Rakosi by reducing his power. Malenkov handed the Hungarian government to Imre Nagy, a former interior minister who had all but retired from public life. Nagy, once a devoted follower of Rakosi, had been disgusted by the party

Interview: The Odyssey of Joseph Magyar*

In some ways, the story of Joseph Magyar embodies the will and tenacity of all Hungarians. Even his last name means Hungarian.

Magyar is a cheerful, friendly man who is now retired and living in Florida. Perhaps his neighbors do not know his background. If they did, they would be impressed at what it took to get him where he is now.

He was born Jozsef Magyar in the eastern Hungarian city of Debrecen on October 28, 1921. His father was a lawyer and an active anticommunist.

During World War II, Magyar was drafted into the Hungarian army and fought on the Eastern Front. He wound up spending three years as a prisoner of war of the Russians. He was lucky to survive that ordeal. More than 70,000 Hungarians did not survive the Russian campaign.

When the Communists came to power in Hungary after the war, Magyar's family was in trouble. His father and mother were jailed. He and his older brother, a major in the Hungarian army, had to work hard to convince the authorities to release their parents.

Magyar and his older brother often discussed the terrible conditions in the country under communism. They had to whisper, even in the family house, because of the presence of a younger brother who was just a schoolboy. In those days, Hungarian teachers encouraged their students to inform the authorities of antigovernment or anticommunist sentiments among family members.

One day, Magyar had had enough. He fled illegally to neighoring Yugoslavia, where he was put in an overcrowded refugee camp. Conditions were so bad there, he made his way to Austria, but was arrested for illegal entry by the British occupation forces in that country. He escaped from the British and crossed into West Germany, where he was again arrested. But the United States military saved him. The Americans needed his language skills: Magyar is fluent in English, French and German. He ended up working as a clerk-typist on a U.S. Air Force base.

Magyar was officially classified as a state-less person, a man without a country. He had only a special United Nations passport. But it was enough to get him entry into the United States in 1949. "I always thought it was easier to get to heaven than to get to America," he says today. In honor of his new home, he Americanized the spelling of his first name to Joseph.

He worked for a time at a copper-smelting plant in New Jersey while living at a local YMCA. He earned enough money to allow him to travel. He lived for a while in Washington, D.C., and then in Seattle. It was the mid-1950s and the Hungarian uprising erupted. His older brother battled alongside the freedom fighters against the Soviets, and was later kicked out of the army for disloyalty.

Magyar was among the first generation in America to learn about computers. He worked as key-punch operator in a Seattle bank in the late 1950s and took courses in the new field of data-processing. He became a United States citizen on January 19, 1961.

Armed with a degree in computer science, he joined the United States Export Import Bank (a federal agency that loans money to foreign interests that want to buy American products) in 1964. Magyar worked at the Eximbank and rose to the major position of director of management systems and data-processing. He retired in 1987.

Magyar has returned to Hungary several times, and he likes the changes he sees there. When asked about the potential for political turmoil in the country, he laughs and notes that Hungarians always disagree with one another. "If two Hungarians are together, you will have three different opinions," he says.

And is there a lesson to be learned from his life? Yes, he answers: "Defeat is not the absolute end. It is a new beginning."

---

*Based on an interview with the author, April 11, 1995

Joseph Magyar.
(Joseph Magyar)

leader's disregard for civil liberties. Rakosi stayed on as the chairman of the Hungarian Workers' Party, but his role and stature were diminished.

The Gathering Storm

Premier Nagy did not remain in office for long. Rakosi forced him out in April 1955, shortly after the Soviet Communist Party removed Malenkov (Nagy's sponsor in Moscow) from power. But during his two-year tenure, Nagy managed to correct some of the harm caused by the party boss. He placed the independent State Security Authority (AVH) under the charge of the interior ministry, giving him at least a minimum of control over the organization. He freed some political prisoners from jail. He redirected government spending away from the heavy industries. He allowed more than 1,500 agricultural cooperatives to break up, and their land to return to private ownership. All in all, Nagy gained the respect of a populace wearied by Rakosi's terror tactics and grandiose, impossible economic schemes.

Nagy's cautiously liberal course emboldened some intellectuals and dissatisfied workers to form a loose-knit coalition known as the Petoefi Club, named after Hungary's 19th-century revolutionary poet, Sandor Petoefi. The club advocated a flexible, reformed communism without a police state. The Petoefites supported a continuation of Nagy's moderate policies, and Nagy's replacement as premier, Andras Hegedus, permitted the club to function.

Rakosi, however, could not leave well enough alone. In June of 1956, he publicly accused Nagy and the Petoefi Club of an anticommunist "conspiracy" against him. The speech was so paranoid, so reminiscent of Stalin, that the Soviet Union removed Rakosi and replaced him with Erno Gero. Typically, the Hungarian Workers' Party announced that Rakosi had stepped down for "health reasons." Gero himself had been a Stalinist. However, he was smart enough to sense the way the wind was blowing in the Kremlin, the seat of the Soviet Communist Party. The heavy-handed approach was out. "De-Stalinization" was in.

Led by Nikita Khrushchev, the new Soviet boss, the Soviet Communist Party was rejecting the police terror of the Stalin era in favor of "Socialist legality." That meant the Soviet security agencies were supposed to respect the civil liberties guaranteed to the people under the Soviet constitution.

In fact, they did not, but they were less openly brutal than they had been under Stalin. De-Stalinization also meant a pretense that Hungary, Poland and the other Soviet "satellites" in Eastern Europe were free to develop their own kinds of communism. In reality, the Kremlin had not stopping pulling the strings. It was just more subtle about it.

Some Eastern Europeans were fooled into believing that a de-Stalinized U.S.S.R. would not intervene if liberal forces challenged their countries' Communist hard-liners. Early in October 1956, there was unrest among workers in Poland that was squashed by that country's security forces. Hungarian university students mobilized in support of the Polish workers and confronted the Hungarian government with a list of demands. The demands included a free press, the withdrawal of Soviet occupation troops, a multiparty political system, guarantees of personal freedom and a return of Imre Nagy as premier.

Anti-Soviet protesters march in Budapest during 1956 uprising. (Wide World Photos)

On the afternoon of October 23, 1956, as many as 100,000 joined a student-led march through Budapest. The security forces confronted the marchers and attempted to break up the demonstration. Mayhem erupted as the demonstrators fought back. A mob of protesters used ropes to pull down a 60-foot-tall bronze statute of Stalin in Dozsa Gyorgy Street. It was the beginning of the Hungarian uprising.

The 1956 Uprising

Experts disagree on whether the majority of Hungarians who took part in the 1956 revolt were seeking Western-style democracy or simply a freer, more responsive type of communism. One thing is certain: they all wanted to be rid of the Soviet chains that bound their country.

Regardless of their aim, people in the West would later call them "freedom fighters." The name stuck to the degree that, throughout the rest of the 1950s, the words "Hungarian" and "freedom fighter" seemed to go together.

On October 24, with no signs of order being restored, the Central Committee of the Workers' Party ousted Andras Hegedus as premier and replaced him with Imre Nagy. The government radio station, Radio Kossuth, appealed for calm, but the appeals were ignored. Workers were now joining students in the street. They were increasingly armed with rifles and home-made gasoline bombs that came to be known as "Molotov cocktails" (sarcastically named after the Soviet foreign minister, Vyacheslav Molotov.) Soviet armored units left their bases throughout Hungary and rushed to Budapest. British journalist Reg Gadney described the fighting this way:

> Soviet tanks thundered through the streets, blocking off bridges and main road intersections. The freedom fighters, moving in small groups, armed with petrol bombs and guns, ran circles around them. If the tank crews made to clamber out, they were met with sniper fire from the windows and rooftops. This game of cat and mouse served as a major delaying tactic until such times as an effective opposing force could be mustered.[5]

The Hungarian army had not yet made an appearance, but its loyalty was determined almost as soon as the Soviets appeared. According to Gadney:

> Many officers and men were in sympathy with the rebels; they showed their support by handing over arms and ammunition. So far, they had not joined the battle. But the appearance of the Soviets, foreigners fighting compatriots, friends and relatives, left them no doubt with whom to side. It had been the Soviets, no less, who had diligently trained the Hungarians to fight invaders on their streets.[6]

Shop workers and patrons watch rebel Hungarian soldiers fire on secret-police units during the 1956 uprising. (Wide World Photos)

High-ranking Soviet Communist officials Anastas Mikoyan and Mikhail Suslov were on the scene in Hungary to make sure order was restored. Under their direction, the Workers' Party dropped Erno Gero as party leader and named Janos Kadar to the post October 25. Rakosi had purged Kadar from the party in 1951, and Kadar had been tortured and imprisoned for three years. Now, he was back and would have a much greater role in the course of Hungarian history than anyone might have imagined at that moment.

Kadar (1912–1989) was a pragmatist, or someone who generally took the most expedient means to an end. He seemed to be less motivated by ideology than by sheer practicality. In public life, he was a humorless, gray man who sought decision by consensus. He was also capable of taking bold action, for good or bad, as Hungarians would soon discover.

Nagy and Kadar pleaded for an end to the violence in radio addresses October 25. Both made vague promises about a negotiated withdrawal of Soviet forces from Hungary and a reorganization of the ruling Workers' Party. (It was renamed the Socialist Workers' Party.) But things were out of control. AVO units fired on demonstrators in Parliament Square in Budapest, killing scores people.

The revolt was not limited to Budapest. By October 26, rebels had taken over the city halls and radio stations of the industrial centers of Gyoer and Miskolc. AVO men shot into a peaceful crowd, killing dozens of people in the town of Magyarovar, about 50 miles from the capital. A mob hunted down the AVO gunmen and literally tore them to pieces.

> Within the hour news of what had happened in Magyarovar reached Budapest and the rebels unleashed their hatred of the AVO with extreme savagery. Innumerable secret policemen were hunted out, lynched or hanged from the branches of trees in the streets and squares. The crowds stood in silence peering at the bloody corpses. Many spat at them. Some AVO men tried to disguise themselves hurriedly in plain clothes. One who had done so failed to change his boots. The boots were spotted. He was chased, caught and lynched.[7]

A mob swarmed into AVO headquarters in the capital and ransacked the place. Another crowd found six unarmed blue-uniformed men hiding in the headquarters of the Greater Budapest Communist Party. Even though they had their hands raised and were begging for mercy, the AVO men were gunned down on the spot. Soon afterward, a pale, frightened woman in civilian dress emerged from the building. Some members of the crowd—believing she was a collaborator or police inform-ant—wanted to kill her. Others argued that she should be spared. They let her live, but only after one angry man knocked her to the ground with the butt of his rifle.

There were many examples of bravery as well as savagery. One Hungarian known as "Uncle Szabo" led a squad of youths that ambushed Soviet tanks with Molotov cocktails. According to one account, the band destroyed as many as 30 tanks, one at a time. Soviet tanks soon learned not to go alone through the streets of Budapest. They began traveling in convoys.

Young people played a prominent role in the uprising. Foreign reporters on the scene saw boys and girls who appeared to be no older than 11 or 12 firing rifles at the Soviets and AVO units.

The uprising wrecked the capital. Tanks fired their cannons into buildings to wipe out snipers. The freedom fighters tore up tram tracks and paving stones to build barricades to halt the Soviet advances. There were dead bodies and burned-out tanks and trucks everywhere.

On October 30, freedom fighters took over Felsopeteny Castle, the AVO prison outside of Budapest. They released the most prominent inmate, Jozsef Cardinal Mindszenty, the Roman Catholic primate of Hungary, who had been jailed under the Rakosi regime. Mindszenty had been in prison for nearly eight years.

Most of the Hungarian army went over to the freedom fighters on October 30, led by a young colonel, Pal Maleter. Premier Nagy promoted Maleter to general and named him deputy defense minister for his courageous action. At the same time, Nagy—with Kadar's apparent support—decided that the only way to save his country from a wholesale Soviet intervention was to appeal to world opinion. In a radio broadcast November 1, he announced Hungary's neutrality and withdrawal from the Warsaw Pact, the Soviet-bloc military alliance. By portraying Hungary as an independent nation, one no longer tied to the U.S.S.R., Nagy hoped that the Western countries might be encouraged to halt the Soviet intervention somehow. He was too late. Massive Soviet military forces, an estimated 250,000 men, swept into Hungary from Czechoslovakia and Ukraine. They were approaching Budapest November 3, when Kadar mysteriously disappeared.

Kadar turned up in the Soviet Union November 4, and declared his support for the Soviet invasion of Hungary. He also announced that he, not Nagy, was Hungary's true leader. It turned out that Kadar had cut a secret deal with the Kremlin: he would become Hungary's leader in return for public backing of the Soviet intervention.

Soviet troops and tanks entered Budapest November 4 and crushed the rebellion by sheer force of numbers. Thousands died in the fighting. And many more thousands fled the city and the country. Droves of Hungarians crossed illegally into neighboring Austria. Nagy, Maleter and several of Nagy's aides were arrested by the Soviets. Cardinal Mindszenty, so recently freed from prison, gained sanctuary in the United States embassy in Budapest.

The Soviets characterized the uprising as a "counterrevolution" by Fascists instigated by the West. The Western nations did little more than lamely protest the U.S.S.R.'s actions. The United States might have wanted to help Hungary, but at the same time it did not want to provoke a confrontation with the Soviets and trigger World War III. Britain and France could not come to Hungary's aid because they were preoccupied in a war with Egypt over the Suez Canal. The United Nations General Assembly condemned the Soviet intervention, but that did not change the situation in any material way.

To no one's surprise, the Soviets installed Janos Kadar as general secretary of the Hungarian Socialist Workers' Party.

According to the official figures of Hungary's Communist government, the uprising left 3,000 dead and 13,000 injured, with 4,000 buildings destroyed. (The true figures were probably much higher.) In addition, as many as 200,000 Hungarians fled the country.

An estimated 2,000 Hungarians were executed in the wake of the uprising. Nagy, Maleter and other prominent rebels were convicted of treason in secret trials. They were put to death in 1958.

The uprising, with all of its tragic consequences, nevertheless reaffirmed the proud, rebellious spirit of the Magyars. As in the revolt against Austrian rule in 1848–49, the Hungarians had risked their lives and their livelihoods to stand up to oppression. Paul Zinner viewed the uprising as an ironic confirmation of a theory of V.I. Lenin, the father of Soviet communism:

According to Lenin, revolutions will occur when the rulers cannot, and the people will not, continue in the old way. In Hungary, both conditions were met.[8]

The New Economic Mechanism

Hungary was a sad, demoralized place for the next decade. The economy was lackluster—no sharp downturns, but no real economic growth, either. The people, still reeling from the 1956 uprising, were low spirited. János Kadar stepped down as premier in 1965, turning the government to Gyula Kallai. However, he remained party leader, and as such he held the most important reins of power.

Worst of all, from the ordinary Hungarian's perspective, the Soviets had about 70,000 soldiers based in Hungary, and there was no sign they would ever leave. Hungary was a member of the Warsaw Pact, the Soviet-led military alliance created in the mid-1950s. The Soviet leadership regarded coalition as essential to the forward defense of the U.S.S.R. itself. Therefore, the Kremlin had no incentive to remove its troops from Hungary or any other part of Eastern Europe.

In short, there seemed to be no genuine hope for positive change, either economically or politically, in Hungary.

The Soviets were willing to give Kadar some leeway since Hungary had been quiet since the uprising. Kadar had demonstrated his allegiance to the Kremlin for a decade, taking the Soviet line in every international dispute with the West. For example, he had firmly backed the U.S.S.R. in its ideological rift with the People's Republic of China in the early 1960s. Similarly, Hungary had followed the Soviet lead in breaking diplomatic relations with Israel after the 1967 Arab-Israeli War. And, in 1968, Hungary had contributed a small contingent to the East-bloc forces that invaded Czechoslovakia to halt the "Prague Spring" liberal reform movement in that country. The Kremlin's trust in Kadar explains why there was no strong Soviet objection to a rather revolutionary idea. Hungarian economists called it "capitalized socialism." To the West, it was "goulash communism." Kadar named it the "New Economic Mechanism."

Basically, the program used limited market mechanisms to revitalize Hungary's economy. Rigid central planning was to give way to flexible guidelines that would take into account the laws of supply and demand. State-owned companies would gain more power to set their own prices and wages. Companies could import from or export to the West with fewer bureaucratic restrictions. Taxes on the profits of money-making state-owned businesses would be lowered.

In a way, the New Economic Mechanism (NEM) was a kind of social contract. According to American experts who studied the plan:

> The Hungarian reform program was designed as a tacit bargain between the government and the people, in which the leaders offered economic incentives and political concessions in return for public cooperation. The promise was that if the people did not actively challenge the political system or the Hungarian ties to the Soviet Union, the leadership would give priority to raising living standards and satisfying consumer needs. In addition, the government offered to relax internal controls and to reorient the country culturally toward the West, lifting barriers to Western travel and interaction. Citizens would no longer have to embrace the system to prosper, only to forswear active opposition.[9]

The NEM was approved by the Central Committee of the Hungarian Socialist Workers' Party in 1966, and it took effect in 1968. One almost immediate result was that Hungary needed to borrow from the West in order to get the capital it needed to begin modernizing its aging industries. Therefore, Hungary's foreign debt took a sharp upturn.

NEM's benefits were soon apparent. Hungarian companies had growing trade contact with the West, mainly Austria and West Germany. Those deals brought consumer goods (televisions, refrigerators, automobiles, clothing etc.) into the country.

Tourism increased dramatically. In 1970, about 6.3 million foreigners visited Hungary. By 1982, the figure was 15.4 million (contributing about 4 percent of the country's foreign-exchange earnings). At the same time, the government permitted about 4 million Hungarians each year to travel abroad; 10 percent were allowed to visit Western countries. Hungary became a favorite travel destination for visitors from the other Communist countries in Eastern Europe. Part of the reason was that consumer goods that were scarce in their own nations could be found in Hungary.

National income rose to 6 percent in 1969 from 4.5 percent in 1968. The value of Hungary's trade also rose by 14 percent. Some two-thirds of Hungary's collective farms began to show a profit beginning in 1970. Real (inflation-adjusted) income rose steadily in the 1970s.

The benefits were real, but so too were the problems associated with NEM. Hungarian companies increasingly had to borrow to get the hard currency to import many Western goods because the postwar native currency, the forint, was uncovertible (it had no value outside of the closed Communist economic sphere). The profits generated by the collective farms were largely due to price increases; in actuality, collective farm production dropped. While real incomes were rising in the late 1970s, industrial productivity was flattening out. By the close of the 1970s, Hungary was in a recession (a prolonged economic slowdown).

One obstacle to the success of the New Economic Mechanism was that the program did not allow for privatization, or turning state-owned enterprises into private companies. Nor did it allow for the private ownership of land. Therefore, the government still subsidized unprofitable industries and state farms, which in turn did not reduce their work forces or take other measures to cut costs.

A second obstacle was the oversized and unwieldy government bureaucracy. Rather than cutting "red tape," government economic rules, decrees and regulations increased under the NEM. For instance, the program allowed workers to form cooperatives to lease factory equipment after normal working hours to produce their own goods. Workers could keep the profits derived from the sale of such goods. But the government monitored the process and required so much complicated paperwork that some workers did not feel it was worth the effort. Those who did, however, raised their income levels above those of ordinary employees.

Another obstacle to the NEM was Hungary's membership in the Council for Mutual Economic Assistance (Comecon), the Soviet-bloc trade alliance. All trade between Comecon nations was either barter (exchanging goods for goods) or denominated in the Soviet currency, the ruble. During the 1970s, up to 35 percent of all Hungarian trade was with the U.S.S.R. Also, Hungary was heavily dependent on Soviet oil to fuel its industries.

Transformation in the 1980s

The entire industrialized world endured a recession in the early 1980s, but the Western countries recovered at the mid-point of the decade. The Communist countries in Europe did not. The economic slowdown dragged through the entire decade. Hungary's economy was at a virtual standstill by 1985. Almost every economic indicator was flat, except for inflation. Real incomes could not keep up with rising prices.

The New Economic Mechanism had gone as far as it could go without radical changes backed by a daring political commitment. In order to revitalize its economy, Hungary would have to take steps to a true market economy like those in the Western nations. One West German writer in Hungary in the late 1980s doubted that the conservative Kadar or the party could go that far.

> A fossilized industrial structure can't be preserved. And that is precisely the regime's dilemma: economic reform is indispensible, but it can't be achieved without political costs. The managers are demanding a free hand, the workers need free unions. The Party would have to surrender a little bit of of its power to each. As long as that thought is unthinkable, Hungarian reform will remain a chimera.[10]

Kadar had attempted to meet some of the demands for change as the economy stagnated. For example, in 1981, Hungary had permitted its citizens to start private businesses of 30 or fewer employees. That gave Hungarians their first small taste of free enterprise under the Communists. In 1985, the government had given workers in 25 percent of state-owned industries the right to elect their own factory managers.

On the political front, Hungary in 1985 was the first Communist country in history to have multi-candidate elections for office. Under the old system, there was only one person running for one office. Voters checked a "yes" or "no" box next to the candidate's name. Usually voters were required to show their marked ballot to a party official before the ballot went into a ballot box.

Granted, under the new voting system, all of the candidates either were once Communists or independents approved beforehand by the Socialist Workers' Party, and the races themselves were for local, not national, offices. Still, for the first time in nearly 40 years, Hungarians were given a choice on the ballot.

The government loosened censorship restrictions in the late 1980s. That opened Hungary to all kinds of literature, films and plays from the Western nations, as well as works banned in other Communist countries. One such work was *The Gulag Archipelago*, a personal account of life in Soviet prison camps by exiled Russian writer Alexander Solzhenitsyn. No other Soviet-bloc nation allowed its people to read about oppression in the U.S.S.R. The government also had eased passport restrictions, making it much easier for Hungarians to travel abroad, including to the West.

In 1987, the government separated the country's five commercial banks from the National Bank of Hungary (the nation's central bank). The same year, the commercial banks were permitted to compete with the central bank in offering deposit accounts to state-owned companies. Hungary was the first Eastern-bloc nation to allow such competition in banking, which is one of the cornerstones of a market economy.

Altogether, Hungary was by far the most politically and economically liberal Communist country in the world by the late 1980s.

Out with the Old, In with the New

The Soviet-bloc Communist parties were led typically by elderly men who found it difficult to deal with the idea of subtantial change. In the 1980s, East Germany's ruler was the cold, rigid Erich Honecker. In Czechoslovakia, it was the scowling, inflexible Gustav Husak. The Bulgarian leader was Marxist hard-liner Todor Zhikov. In Romania, dictator Nicolae Ceausescu reigned with almost God-like authority.

In comparison to his fellow East-bloc leaders, Hungary's Janos Kadar was a liberal. At least, Kadar was willing to try daring approaches to solve his country's problems. The New Economic Mechanism and the personal freedoms allowed in Hungary were evidence that he was not quite like the other Eastern European party bosses.

Yet by 1988, Kadar reached the limit of his liberalism. He was 75 years old and simply could not go farther toward reform than he already had without violating his life-long principles. Younger members of the Socialist Workers' Party, people in their 40s and 50s, realized that Kadar

Premier Karoly Grosz speaks with Janos Kadar (right) at a special party conference in 1988. Grosz replaced Kadar as the Commuinist leader a few hours after the photo was taken. (Wide World Photos)

was not the man to lead Hungary into the 1990s. The country's problems were too large.

At the end of 1987, Hungary's foreign debt stood at about $17 billion, the highest per capita (per person) in the Eastern bloc. According to official government figures, 30,000 Hungarians were unemployed in early 1988, some 10,000 more than in 1987.

The Socialist Workers held a special party conference in May 1988 to discuss the problems and the party's future direction. Observers expected some personnel changes in the Politburo (the party's top policy-making body) because such changes were routine in Communist countries. What observers did not expect was that Kadar would be forced out as the party leader. That happened on May 22, the third and last day of the meeting. The 1,000 delegates—party officials, students, workers and intellectuals—voted Kadar out of power. They handed the party leadership to Karoly Grosz, who was then Hungary's premier.

Kadar had been party general secretary for 32 years, ever since he had betrayed Imre Nagy during the 1956 uprising. The delegates softened the blow somewhat by appointing Kadar to the presidency of the Socialist Workers' Party. However, that was largely a ceremonial position. He had no real authority.

The changeover to Grosz apparently came as a surprise to Kadar. There had been no prior indication he was ready or willing to step down. But he accepted his demotion with a sad grace.

Kadar's removal was not all. The delegates threw out 40 percent of the Central Committee (the large party parliament), and ousted seven Kadar allies from the Politburo on May 22.

Grosz, 57 at the time of the conference, was the first Hungarian Communist leader ever to spend his entire life under communism. He could barely remember when Hungary was not a Marxist country. However, he was not wedded to doctrine or ideology. If anything, Grosz (like Kadar in his younger years) was a pragmatist, a person willing to take whatever steps he deemed necessary.

If Grosz resembled any Communist political figure, it was Mikhail S. Gorbachev of the Soviet Union. Gorbachev had become the Soviet Communist Party leader in 1985, following to power a parade of sick old men. From the start, he dedicated himself to reforming the creaky, antiquated Soviet political and economic systems.

Like Gorbachev in the U.S.S.R., Grosz and his allies in the party leadership did not start out to transform Hungary into a capitalist democracy. And like Gorbachev, Grosz would find out that once certain political and economic forces are set in motion, they gather their own momentum. Both men seemed to believe that their reasonableness, moderation and political savvy could somehow keep the forces in check.

There had been those in the Soviet Communist Party, like Moscow party chief Boris N. Yeltsin, who pushed Gorbachev to make faster and more radical reforms than Gorbachev wanted. (Yeltsin went on to become the president of Russia in June 1991.) In Hungary, the radical reformers were embodied in the so-called "reform circles" of the Socialist Workers' Party. The circles' most prominent figure was Minister of State Imre Pozsgay.

It was the reform circles that pushed Grosz and the party, in November 1988, into giving official status to independent political organizations like the Hungarian Democratic Union. The union described itself as a "democratic, intellectual and political movement." It really was, in essence, a forerunner to the non-Communist opposition parties that would spring up in Hungary within a year.

By granting official status to the union and other such "movements," Grosz hoped to give Hungarians an outlet for political free expression without actually having the Communists give up their monopoly on political power. However, the move inevitably led to talk of a true multiparty system in Hungary. That is what the reform circles wanted.

The circles also wanted a Western-style market economy in Hungary. They wanted Hungary to be a neutral country, with no Soviet troops on its soil. They wanted an official reappraisal of the 1956 uprising, which, according to Hungary's history books, had been a revolt by "counterrevolutionary" traitors swayed by the West. Thanks in part to Mikhail Gorbachev, the Hungarian radical reformers eventually would get everything they wanted.

Grosz and Gorbachev

In March 1989, Karoly Grosz visited the Soviet Union and held private discussions with Gorbachev. According to Grosz, the Soviet leader promised that his country would not interfere with any political reforms in Hungary or elsewhere in Eastern Europe. The pledge was an explicit renunciation of the "Brezhnev Doctrine" (named after former Soviet leader Leonid Brezhnev). The doctrine asserted the right of the Soviet Union to intervene militarily to preserve Communist regimes. Brezhnev had formulated the doctrine to justify the Soviet-led 1968 invasion of Czechoslovakia.

Gorbachev in effect gave Grosz a "green light" to proceed with his reforms without fear of a repeat of the 1956 Soviet invasion. He also took away a major excuse Grosz and the Hungarian moderates might have used for blocking radical reforms.

In truth, reforms had been moving along in Hungary even before Grosz went to Moscow. But they had proceeded while everyone in Hungary glanced nervously easterward to see if there were any Soviet tanks on the horizon.

A month before Grosz's trip, the Central Committee of the Hungarian Socialist Workers' Party approved in principle the creation of a multiparty political system in Hungary. At the same time, a party historical committee announced that the 1956 revolt was a "popular uprising" against a dictatorial regime, rather than a counterrevolution.

The party removed Janos Kadar as its president in May 1989, explaining that he was no longer physically fit enough to hold the post. (Kadar died of respiratory and circulatory problems on July 6, at age 77. He was given a state funeral eight days later that was attended by 10,000 people.)

On June 16, 1989, an estimated 250,000 people gathered in Heroes Square in Budapest to view six flag-draped coffins. Five of the caskets contained the remains of Imre Nagy and four other leading figures of the 1956 uprising. The sixth coffin was empty; it symbolized all of the other dead freedom fighters. Nagy and his key associates—General Pal Maleter, Jozsef Szilagyi, Geza Losonczy and Miklos Gimes— had been buried in an unmarked mass grave in Budapest. All but Losonczy, who died in prison while awaiting trial, were tried in secret and executed for treason. They were reburied with honors June 16 after the Budapest ceremony. Several speakers at the ceremony described the uprising as a revolution. Writer Tibor Meray made an emotional speech at Nagy's gravesite. He denounced the premier's executioners as "common criminals who are among us today," meaning men who still held high posts in the Communist Party. "But," Meray added, "we must not seek revenge. Their punishment is that they see what is happening today."

After reviewing their trials, Hungary's Supreme Court ruled in July 1989 that Nagy and his aides were unjustly accused of treason and illegally put on trial. At last, the heroes of 1956 were officially "rehabilitated."

The International Scene

The reform fever sweeping Hungary was not limited to domestic affairs. In May 1989, the country removed the barbed-wire fence that separated Hungary from neutral Austria. Thus, Hungary became the first Eastern-bloc nation to open a border with a non-Communist country.

U.S. president George Bush paid a state visit to Hungary on July 11, 1989, bringing with him a modest package of economic aid. Hungarians were elated by the visit. He was the first American president ever to set foot in the country.

Also in the summer of 1989, thousands of East German tourists in Hungary refused to return to their own country. At the time, East Germany was experiencing political turmoil, with masses of protesters in the streets demanding democratic reforms. East Germany had one of the most hard-line Communist regimes in the Soviet bloc.

Most of the East German vacationers in Hungary were young adults with children. They simply did not wish to go home. After initially trying to convince them to return to their country, the Hungarian government decided not to forcibly send them back. Instead, Hungary opened discussions with West Germany and Austria on the possibility of those two countries granting political asylum to the East Germans.

Between September 11, 1989 and October 1, 1989, Hungary allowed as many as 30,000 East Germans to cross the border into Austria. From Austria, they were taken to West Germany for political asylum. East Germany was furious. Under a 20-year-old agreement, Hungary was supposed to block any attempt by East Germans to reach the West. In effect, Hungary had thumbed its nose at its Central European comrade.

Communists Dump Marxism-Leninism

The Socialist Workers' Party stunned the world October 7, 1989, when it renounced Marxism-Leninism and adopted democratic socialism as its guiding principle. It also renamed itself the Hungarian Socialist Party.

It was also the first time in history that a ruling Communist party turned away from its fundamental ideology. Marxism, developed by 19th-century German social theorists Karl Marx and Fredrich Engels, espoused the belief that a natural process of economic class struggle would inevitably replace bourgeois (middle-class) capitalism with socialism (an economic system in which all property is held in common, eliminating class differences). Lenin, a Russian revolutionary, argued that the proletariat (working-class) masses of the world could gain political and economic power only through revolution.

Marxism-Leninism was the framework ideology of all of the Communist nations. In Hungary, the party entirely abandoned Leninism and backed away from such rigid Marxist concepts as "class struggle." A majority of members even refused to call themselves Marxists; they preferred the less historically weighted designation of "Socialists." At the same time, the party publicly committed itself to Western-style democracy.

The changes came at a special party congress (a high-level meeting) in Budapest. The gathering had been called to detemine the direction of party, and to fashion a new image for the party with national elections expected in 1990.

The shift to democratic socialism was guided by Rezso Nyers, the party president. It was a defeat for both the party's moderate Communists, under Karoly Grosz, and its radical reformers, under Imre Pozsgay. Pozsgay wanted the party to turn liberal democratic (center-left on the political spectrum, to the right of Socialists). Grosz, who remained a faithful Marxist, was disgusted. He criticized the delegates for giving up unspecified "Communist values," and said he wanted nothing to do with the new Socialist Party.

Constitution Amended

On October 18, 1989, the National Assembly amended the country's 1949 constitution to pave the way for multiparty national elections. Among the changes, the deputies:

- Eliminated the Socialist Workers' monopoly on political power, and removed all references in the charter to the party's "leading role" in Hungary
- Stated: "Political parties may be freely established and may freely function"
- Renamed the country the "Hungarian Republic." The Communist-era designation in use since 1949, the "People's Republic of Hungary," was abandoned
- Codified civil liberties, such as freedom of speech, freedom of religion, freedom of association and the right to peaceably assemble.

Hungarian Republic Proclaimed

An estimated 80,000 people gathered in front of the parliament building on October 23, 1989 to hear Acting President Matyas Szuros proclaim Hungary a free republic. The event was nationally televised. The date marked the 33rd anniversary of the 1956 uprising. The building was decked with a giant portrait of Imre Nagy and a huge banner that read: "Freedom, Independence."

Even though Hungary was still part of the Eastern bloc, and Soviet troops were still on Hungarian soil, the ceremony gave its people a heady sense that true freedom was close, indeed that it was an unstoppable process. October 23 would from that day on be celebrated as a national holiday.

The 1990 Elections

Hungary held its first free elections since the end of World War II in 1990. The voting was to fill the 386-seat National Assembly. The election was in two stages: the main voting on March 25, and runoff voting April 8 for races that had been left undecided.

An estimated 7 million Hungarians cast ballots. Some 1,600 candidates representing 54 political parties took part. When all the votes were tallied, the conservative Hungarian Democratic forum captured 42.7 percent of the votes, or 165 seats. That was more than any other party, but it was not an absolute majority. In other words, all of the other winning parties together held more seats than the forum.

The liberal Alliance of Free Democrats finished second, with 23.8 percent of the vote, or 92 seats. The Independent Smallholders' Party got 11.1 percent of the vote (43 seats). The ruling Socialists (former Communists) ended up fourth, with 8.5 percent, or 33 seats. The Christian Democrats came in fifth, with 5.4 percent, for 21 seats.

Because the Democratic Forum lacked an absolute majority, it formed a ruling coalition with the other major right-of-center parties, the Smallholders and the Christian Democrats. The Free Democrats and the Socialists made up the main parliamentary opposition.

More than 80,000 people gather before the parliament building to hear Hungary proclaimed a free republic on October 23, 1989. (Wide World Photos)

The forum campaigned on a platform of ridding Hungary of the last vestiges of communism, but also of maintaining Hungary's links with existing Soviet-bloc organizations. (The Warsaw Pact military alliance and the Comecon trade alliance still existed, and Hungary still belonged to them.) However, the forum made no secret of its pro-Western orientation.

The elections were influenced by anti-Magyar riots in the Transylvania region of neighboring Romania. The forum, more than any other Hungarian party, capitalized on the strong anti-Romanian feelings in Hungary. Forum candidates hinted, but did not say outright, that Hungary should go to war with Romania to protect the lives of the ethnic Hungarians in Transylvania (see p. 125).

Anti-Semitism, too, played a role in the election. The Free Democrats, a party with a high number of Jewish members, accused the forum of spurring anti-Jewish feelings among voters. The forum denied the accusation.

The forum's Jozsef Antall, a 58-year-old historian, became Hungary's first post-Communist premier on May 3, 1990. A new era moving toward democracy had begun.

NOTES

1. Paul E. Zinner, *Revolution in Hungary* (New York: Columbia University Press, 1962), p. 114.
2. Ibid., pp. 116–117.
3. Joerg K. Hoensch, *A History of Modern Hungary: 1867–1986* (New York: Longman, Inc., 1988), p. 192.
4. Paul E. Zinner, *Revolution in Hungary* (New York: Columbia University Press, 1962), p. 115.
5. Reg Gadney, *Cry Hungary!: Uprising 1956* (New York: Atheneum, 1986), p. 53.
6. Ibid.
7. Ibid., p. 89.
8. Paul E. Zinner, *Revolution in Hungary* (New York: Columbian University Press, 1962), p. 359.
9. Kerry Dumbaugh and Frances T. Miko, *Gorbachev's Reform Strategy: Comparisons with the Hungarian and Chinese Experience,* Congressional Research Service report number 87-813 F. (Washington, D.C., 1987), p. 7.
10. Hans Magnus Enzensberger, *Europa, Europa* (New York: Random House, Inc., 1989), p. 107.

PART II

HUNGARY TODAY

4

Politics and Government

*I*n the turbulent years between 1989 and 1991, the world marveled at the collapse of communism in Eastern Europe and the breakup of the Soviet Union into 15 separate countries. Yet, by the end of 1995, former Communists either ruled, or were posed to rule, a majority of the new democries. Hungary was part of the startling trend: in 1994, after four years of conservative government, Hungarians elected reformed Communists to power.

On the face of it, Hungary—once the most liberal of the Soviet-bloc countries—seemed to be the least likely to elect a government of former Marxists. Several factors help to explain the election results. The death in 1993 of Premier Jozsef Antall, who had embodied a pro-Western, free-market philosophy, left a political vacuum. Scandals and allegations of corruption in Antall's government had turned many voters away from the ruling Democratic Forum. But perhaps the biggest factor was widespread dissatisfaction over economic reform, which had led to high unemployment and a general decline in the standard of living.

Hungary, like most of the countries of Eastern Europe, has little experience with democracy. For most of the nation's history, it has been ruled by kings and emperors and by coercive governments of the right and left. The post-Communist era has encouraged the creation of many political parties, including ones on the political extremes. But the transition to democracy has been relatively smooth, and there seems to be little sentiment in the country for a return to despotism.

Parliamentary Democracy

Americans, particularly young Americans, are usually familiar with only one form of democratic government—the federal system used in the United States since its birth as a nation. But Hungary and most of the world's other democratic countries, new and old, use the parliamentary system.

Under the federal system, the executive branch (headed by the president) and the legislative branch (Congress) are separate parts of the government. The parliamentary system combines the executive and legislative branches.

Members of a parliament, or national legislature, are elected by the voters. The party that wins a clear-cut majority of seats (that is, its members can out-vote members of all other parties represented in parliament combined) has the right to form a new government. If one party has a plurality—it holds a majority of seats, but can be out-voted by the other parties together—it might form a ruling coalition, or partnership, with one or more other parties in order to obtain a voting majority in parliament.

The majority party or coalition has the power to designate a premier (sometimes called a prime minister) to head the government. The premier, in turn, chooses a cabinet of officials (who are always fellow members of parliament) to head the government's major departments or ministries.

In the United States, the president is both the head of government and the head of state. In Hungary and the other parliamentary democracies, the premier is only the head of government. Hungary's president—who is picked by parliament—is the head of state; an official who embodies national unity, but who has mainly ceremonial powers and duties.

Members of Hungary's parliament, the 386-seat Orszaggyules (National Assembly), are elected to four-year terms. At the end of the four years, new national elections must be held. But, in Hungary, as in countries with similar systems, the government (the premier and his or her cabinet) can be forced out of power at any time by a simple majority vote of the members of parliament. For that reason, frequent changes of government can be common in some parliamentary democracies.

The Death of a Leader

On December 12, 1993, the longest-serving leader in post-Communist Eastern Europe died quietly in a Budapest hospital. He was Premier Jozsef Antall, the man who had directed Hungary's first steps in the transition from communism to democracy. Antall, 61, had taken office on May 3, 1990. No other country in the former Soviet bloc could boast of having a head of government in power as long as Antall.

Antall's death came as no surprise, since he had been seriously ill for several years. Nevertheless, most Hungarians were stunned and saddened by the news of his passing. He had personally symbolized the emergence of a new era.

The premier died of non-Hodgkin's lymphoma, a type of cancer. In spite of his poor health, Antall had been known as a workaholic. He often arrived at his office before 8 A.M. and worked until late in the evening. He carried out a vigorous schedule of meetings, speeches and official travel. Antall's energy, earnest manner and strong conservative convictions gained him the respect of many Western leaders, including United States president George Bush.

The Hungarian press—which was not known for its gentle treatment of politicians—respected Antall's privacy so much that it declined to raise the issue of his health for as long as he was in power. Antall himself refused to discuss the matter in public. The government would not reveal the names of the premier's doctors or his course of treatment.

The premier's passing left the ruling Democratic Forum without a leader of Antall's stature. Hungarian President Arpad Goncz named Peter Boross, who had been the interior minister in Antall's cabinet, to the post of acting premier. Boross served as the head of government until the national elections in the spring of 1994.

The Ex-Communists Return

A jubilant crowd gathered at the Budapest former headquarters of the Communists on the night of May 29, 1994. They surrounded a slender, smiling middle-aged man. The celebrants wanted to slap the man on the back or hug him, but they could not. The center of attention, Gyula Horn, was wearing a head and neck brace. He had been in a car accident a few weeks earlier.

Horn was the leader of the Hungarian Socialist Party, which had once been the mighty Socialist Workers' (Communist) Party. The Socialists had just won the 1994 national elections, and Horn was poised to be Hungary's next premier. Horn, 62, had been a life-long Communist and had served in an auxiliary police unit that had helped to put down the 1956 Hungarian uprising. But he had gone on to become an internationally respected foreign minister in the 1980s, and had played a key role in opening Hungary borders in the late 1980s. Horn had been one of the leaders of the reform wing of the Socialist Workers' Party.

Now that the ex-Communists were back in power, what could the nation expect? Horn took pains to calm any fears that his party would try to halt the advance of capitalism and democracy in Hungary. He spoke of "reconciliation," telling one observer: "Let us not deal with ideologies. Those with decent intentions have nothing to fear."[1]

The 1994 national elections, held in two stages (May 8 and May 29), constituted the first nationwide vote since the 1990 balloting that had brought the Democratic Forum to power. The voting was to fill the 386-seat Orszaggyules (National Assembly). Under the National Assembly system, the party with the most seats was empowered to form a government, with the party leaders as the nation's premier.

More than 60 percent of eligible voters cast ballots in each of the two stages. The Socialists captured a total of 209 seats, giving them a clear majority. The Alliance of Free Democrats finished second, with a total of 70 seats. The Democratic Forum ended up third, with 38 seats. The rest of the seats were divided mainly between the Independent Smallholders' and Civic Party, the Christian Democrats and the Alliance of Young Democrats.

Since the Socialists had an outright majority, they had no need to form a coalition government. Yet they invited the Free Democrats to be a coalition partner. The leader of the Free Democrats, Gabor Kuncze, initially rejected the offer. Less than a month later, he changed his mind and accepted.

From the Socialists' point of view, the coalition would give their party credibility and calm fears of a return to communism in Hungary. The Free Democrats gained power; they never before had been in a government. The two parties together could muster 279 votes in the National Assembly.

Several factors accounted for the sweeping Socialist victory. First, there was public disaffection with economic reform. Since the last elections, in 1990, Hungarians had seen an overall decline in their standard of living. Although wages had increased, high prices had eroded purchasing power. And tens of thousands of people were out of work. Many voters, especially blue-collar workers and the elderly on pensions, yearned for a return of the economic stability of the Communist era.

The ruling Democratic Forum, along with the Free Democrats, also had been implicated in a major scandal. It seems that the two parties in secret had sold office space that had been granted them by the government privatization (the selling of government-owned properties and industries to individuals and private businesses) agency, the State Property Agency. The transaction—which had not been reported in the parties' financial statements—had been revealed by two newspapers in 1993. Both parties claimed that they had not broken any laws. The national law on party financing apparently contained so many loopholes that the forum and Young Democrats could not be held accountable. The parties shrugged off the scandal, but it angered many voters. They viewed the two parties as self-serving pirates.

The Socialist–Free Democrat coalition was little more than a marriage of convenience. The two parties do not share the same philosophies, particularly on the matter privatization. The Socialists appear to be committed to slowing privatization, while the Free Democrats want it to continue apace.

A clash over economic reform was inevitable. It happened in 1995, when the Free Democrats threatened to quit the coalition over what they viewed as Premier Horn's political interference in the privatization process (see p. 107). The rift was eventually smoothed over, but ever since the partnership has remained shaky.

Major Party Profiles

There are six major political parties, and scores of minor ones, in Hungary. Unlike in the United States, Hungarian voters do not register as members

The state-owned Forum Hotel (right) in Budapest was part of a political dispute over privatization in 1995. (Hungarian Tourist Board)

of one party or another. Any Hungarian citizen 18 years of age or older can vote in any election.

The Socialists, under Horn, campaigned on a platform of softening the effects of economic reform on ordinary Hungarians. However, they vowed support for a market economy and respect for private property. The Socialists also promised to control government spending. The party drew votes from all economic levels, but its base of power was the working class, particularly unionized workers. They were the ones suffering the most under the economic transition.

Hungary's Socialists are roughly the equivalent of the left-wing British Labour Party or the German Social Democrats. They all stand for capitalism balanced by strong social-welfare programs and strict government regulations.

The Free Democrats resemble in ideology the U.S. Democratic Party or Britain's Liberal Democrats. Gabor Kuncze's party is center-left on social issues, but is a firm supporter of moderately regulated capitalism.

The Free Democrats are the spiritual sons and daughters of the non-Communist leftist intellectuals of Hungary during the 1920s through the 1940s. Many of the party members are Jewish, and the party appears to have the financial backing of Hungary's Jewish community. However, the party is nondenominational and takes no stand on religion except to endorse freedom of worship. The Free Democrats also have a power base among Hungary's growing middle class and entreprenuers.

The Democratic Forum is right of center, like the U.S. Republican Party, the British Conservative Party, and Germany's Christian Democrats. It attracts older, conservative Hungarians. The forum advocates free-market capitalism, a strong military, Christian values and Hungarian traditions. Many of its supporters—like Premier Antall—are Roman Catholics.

The Christian Democrats are more conservative and more narrowly focused than the Democratic Forum, their senior partner in the first post-Communist government. The party draws most of its support from Hungary's Roman Catholic community, and regards itself as the defender of the church's interests in Hungary. Among other things, the Christian Democrats favor a full return of, or compensation for, the land confiscated from the church by the Communists.

The Young Democrats constitute Hungary's hippest major party. They perhaps most resemble the Green parties of Western Europe. (The Green parties were formed by young people in the 1980s on a pro-environment, antiwar platform.) The Young Democrats initially barred anyone over the age of 35 from joining their party. They support personal freedom, free enterprise, European unity, peace and rock 'n' roll. Naturally, the Young Democrats appeal to large segments of Hungary's youth.

The Independent Smallholders are the self-proclaimed descendants of the same party that held power in Hungary briefly after World War II and before the Communist takeover. Their power base is among the farmers in rural Hungary, but they have expanded into the cities as well. The Smallholders are right-wing populists, in that they advocate a farmer-worker alliance to achieve political power.

The New Nazis

The fall of communism, and the advent of economic transition, has spurred the growth of extreme-right political parties and of neo-Fascist skinhead movements in Hungary and elsewhere in Eastern Europe. The parties and movements attract people at the bottom of the economic ladder: jobless workers and working-class youths. They are people who do not see how they fit in with the new economic order.

Although the parties and movements differ in some respects, they all espouse radical nationalism. They hate Jews and foreigners, and believe that Hungary has a right to take back the bordering lands it lost after World War I. They admire Ferenc Szalasi, the founder of Hungary's Fascist Arrow Cross movement. (Szalasi was executed in 1946.)

The growth of the extremists in many ways is a reflection of events on a higher political level. In August 1992, Istvan Csurka, one of the leaders of the Democratic Forum, published a controversial essay in which he accused Jews and Communists of plotting against Hungary. He also suggested that Hungary expand its borders to include the lands it had once ruled. Premier Antall had been slow to criticize Csurka.

Csurka and some his followers were forced out of the Democratic Forum in 1993. They formed their own party, the Hungarian Justice and Life Party. Thus far, it has not achieved much political success.

Hungary has two registered political parties that are by all accounts neo-Fascist. One is the Hungarian National Socialist Action Group, based in the city of Gyoer. The other is the World National Popular Rule Party

(WNPRP), based in the working-class Angyalfold district of Budapest. The latter party is led by Albert Szabo, a Hungarian-born laborer who spent part of his life in Australia. According to one Western newspaper:

> Szabo described [the party's] goal as the protection of the interests of Hungarians, whom he considers culturally superior to all other nations. The WNPRP advocates restricting the number of minorities [Jews and Gypsies] at universities and at places of employment to their proportion in the population at large.[2]

Skinheads, or young neo-Nazis, first emerged in Hungary in the 1970s. Police currently estimate that there are 300–400 active skinheads in the country, with about 3,000 sympathizers. They are prone to violence. A knowledgeable observer of the skinhead scene reports:

> They blame Jews, Gypsies, and foreigners for Hungary's problems, and in recent years the number of incidents in which they have beaten up Asian and African students, Jews and Gypsies has increased, receiving great publicity. In the last few months, there have been a series of bomb threats against Jewish schools, and Jewish cemeteries and a synagogue were desecrated. Jewish leaders attributed the attacks to skinheads and expressed alarm that the movement was targeting Jewish institutions.[3]

The Extreme Left

The fall of communism left Marxist hard-liners dazed and disheartened. They could not go along with the reformed Communists (today's Socialists), so they formed their own, new parties. The two best-known of the new extreme-left parties are the Labor Party (LP) and the Hungarian Socialist Workers' Party (the name of the former Communist party). Of course, both parties oppose capitalism. Western reporter Edith Oltay sums up the Labor Party this way:

> The LP portrays itself as the only party in Hungary that represents the interests of workers and peasants. Defining the LP as "the party of the ordinary people," its leader, Gyula Thurmer, claims to speak in the name of those who failed to benefit from the change of

regime—the unemployed, pensioners, and the young. The majority of the LP's supporters are elderly people who live in the provinces and have a low educational level. Most of its supporters are motivated by the feeling that "it was better in the old days. . . . "[4]

Dealing with the Communist Past

Although some Hungarians have clamored for Communist-era officials to be put on trial, a majority of the country appears to be against the move. The opponents believe that such trials would needlessly reawaken hatreds over such issues as the use of ordinary citizens as secret police informants.

As of the end of 1995, no Communist-era officials in Hungary had been prosecuted for major crimes. That is because in 1992 the Constitutional Court—the highest court in the country—overturned a new law that would have permitted Communist leaders to be brought to trial.

In 1991, the National Assembly passed a law lifting a Communist-era statute of limitations (a legal time limit on prosecutions) on such crimes as murder and treason if those crimes were committed in the name of Marxism. In other words, the Communists protected themselves from possible future prosecution.

By throwing out the statute of limitations, the Democratic Forum hoped to bring surviving Communists to justice for their past actions. President Arpad Goncz opposed the move. Goncz, who had been imprisoned by the Communists, believed that criminal trials would be vindictive and might divide the country.

The Constitutional Court criticized the 1991 law as "vague" and "unreliable." The court added:

> We cannot judge a previous period of time from the point of view of the present. We must make laws in advance of a crime and not afterward.[5]

In another development during 1992, the National Assembly passed a law voiding the convictions of all persons prosecuted by the Communists for political crimes between 1963 and 1989. The crimes included conspiracy, rebellion and illegal emigration (leaving Hungary without official permission).

Politics and the Economy

Hungarian politics is not consumed with righting the wrongs of the Communist past. Although the successive post-Communist governments have established mechanisms for, say, compensation for confiscated property, such issues are largely dealt with by the national courts.

The number-one political issues have to do with economic policy. Should major state-owned industries be privatized, and if so how quickly? How much of the economy should be owned by foreigners? What laws are needed to facilitate the growth of the private sector? Can the government substantially reduce spending without destroying the social-welfare "safety net"? What steps can the government take to make Hungary's exports more competitive with the products of other countries? These are the issues that presently consume Hungarian politicians.

Hungary, like other post-Communist nations of Eastern Europe, lacks the money to reshape itself in a world with new realities. Many seemingly noneconomic political issues—such as protecting the borders against smuggling, rebuilding the military and cleaning up the environment—come down to two questions: How much money will the task cost? Can the government afford it?

NOTES

1. *New York Times,* May 30, 1994, Sec A, p. 3.
2. Edith Oltay, "Extremist Politics in Hungary," *RFE/RL Research Reports,* April 22, 1994, p. 56.
3. Ibid., p. 57.
4. Ibid., p. 60.
5. *Facts On File World News Digest,* March 19, 1992, p. 196A3.

5

Economy and Trade

*H*ungary began the era of economic transformation in the early 1990s as the shining star of the former Soviet bloc. Since then, the star has lost some of its luster.

When looking at Hungary's economy during its transition, an observer is tempted to ask: is the glass half empty or half full? On the one hand, Hungary has attracted more foreign investment than any of the other ex-Communist nations in Eastern Europe. On the other hand, government spending seems to be out of control. On the one hand, new businesses are growing at an astounding rate. On the other, more than half a million Hungarians are out of work.

What happened? Hungarian leaders perhaps expected too much from foreign investment, which they believed would cushion the shocks of taking the nation from Marxist central planning to a free-market economy. Today, the government still spends large sums on subsidies to money-losing state-owned businesses while politicians bicker over the pace of privatization. The economy is far too dependent on borrowed money. And the average Hungarian wonders why so many goods are priced beyond his or her reach.

The ultimate aim of Hungary's economic policies is for the country to one day be part of an integrated Europe. The nation's leaders forsee a day when Hungary's exports will flow freely across the continent, with little or no trade barriers. Until that day and its promises of widespread prosperity arrive, Hungarians will probably continue to endure the bruises of reform.

The Wizard of Ozd

Picture a huge steel plant in Ozd, a small town in northeastern Hungary near the border with Slovakia. The complex has been in existence since 1804, when it manufactured brass military cannons. At its height, in the 1960s, the Ozd operation employed more than 14,000 steelworkers. Shifts worked around the clock amid searing blast furnaces and clanging machinery. The government-owned complex was one of the largest single employers in Hungary. And, it was a very profitable enterprise.

Now picture the same Ozd plant in 1994. The entire complex is deserted except for two sections. Nothing now emerges from the tall chimneys that used to belch black smoke 24 hours a day. Most of its machines are silent and rusting. Most of the workers have been laid off. In one of the only two operating sections of the complex, about 1,000 remaining workers are employed processing scrap steel for meager wages. But in the other section, about 700 well-paid employees are turning out clever, useful metal products for export all over Europe.

In a way, the Ozd plant is the story of Hungary's troubled transition from the "capitalized socialism" of the 1970s to the market economy of the 1990s. It is a story of both abject failure and daring success.

The steel complex, like most of Hungary's industries, had fallen on hard times in the late 1970s through the 1980s. That had been a period of recession (severe economic slowdown) and lagging productivity. During that time, the plant retained most of its work force even though it was losing millions of dollars a year. Aging equipment and obsolete work rules had contributed to the problem. The plant no longer was competitive, even in the closed economic sphere of the Soviet bloc.

Then, in 1988, a savior of sorts appeared on the scene. He was Janos Petrenko, an ambitious former worker who had dreams of becoming an entrepreneur, or risk-taking business owner. This was a time when the reformed Communists were pushing the older, conservative Communists out of power. Petrenko used his charm and gift of gab to convince the government to sell him one section of the Ozd plant for about $2 million. A government-owed bank loaned him the money. Petrenko turned the small section into a private company, Peko Steel Industrial Works. He fired the entire management team of the section he had inherited from the government. At the same time he raised the number of workers in the section to 647 from 445. Among the new employees were creative people hired to design new products.

"If we were going to survive," he recalled in 1993, "we had to have new products. . . . The big problem with socialism was that people were embedded in tradition, old concepts, old ideas. I wanted fresh thinking."[1]

In 1990, Petrenko was struggling to make enough money to pay his employees and to make his loan payments. That year, another apparent savior showed up. A German steel company purchased the rest of the Ozd complex (excluding Petrenko's company) in hopes of turning a quick profit. The Germans believed that they could use the cheap labor at the plant—Hungarian steelworkers earned much less than German steelworkers—to undercut the shaky steel markets in other parts of Eastern Europe. But they could not find any new markets in the region. And the Ozd workers could not adjust quickly to the rigid new work rules imposed by the Germans to increase efficiency. The plant continued to lose millions of dollars.

Peko Steel Industrial Works turned its first profit in 1991. Rather than trying to go head-to-head with the major steel manufacturers of Europe, Petrenko's company concentrated on finding niches ("vacuum areas" in his terminology) for metal products that no one else was turning out. One such product was an inexpensive portable stove that burned sawdust, cherry pits and other waste materials. He focused initially on the Hungarian and Eastern European markets, setting the groundwork for exports to Western Europe as well.

Meanwhile, by the close of 1991, the Germans had decided to cut their losses on the Ozd facility. They declared bankruptcy and withdrew their remaining investments in the complex. More than 12,000 steelworkers lost their jobs. The relative handful of employees that were not laid off were left to eke out a living recycling scrap metal. One of the remaining workers, Laszlo Nagy, had worked at the complex for 25 years. Speaking with some bitterness, he told a reporter in 1994, "The Germans shut down the furnaces. They didn't do anything for us. Under the old system, we had security. Today we live from day to day."[2]

Peko Steel experienced a downturn in 1992, but bounced back in 1993 to do an estimated $22 million in business. Petrenko increased and diversified his product line to include electronic motors and steel rims for buses and trucks. His company also created a retail division, opening several Western-style "superstores." Petrenko also incorporated a subsidiary, Peko Corporation, in the U.S. state of Wisconsin. By incorporating in the U.S., Petrenko made it easier to export his products to America and to have access to American commercial technology. In addition, Petrenko cut a deal with Ukraine that gave Peko Steel 50 percent ownership of a steel plant in the Ukrainian capital of Kiev.

Hungary is full of new entrepreneurs like Janos Petrenko. They are men and women with the courage and insight to take advantage of the freedoms offered by the fledgling market economy. There is Peter Zwack, the head of Zwack Unicum Ltd., a leading distiller of alcoholic beverages. Zwack comes from an aristocratic family that fled Hungary in 1948. He returned in 1988 and started his company (in partnership with the German distiller Underberg Group) by selling a liqueur based on a secret recipe that had been in his family for generations. The liqueur, called Unicum, quickly became one of Hungary's favorite alcoholic drinks.

Gabor Szeles is another very successful entreprenuer. He is a former electrical engineer who founded Videoton, a private company that has become the largest consumer-electronics business in Eastern Europe. Szeles' rapid rise to the status of corporate mogul is legendary. Videoton is now entering the fields of computers and telecommunications equipment.

Hungarian-born George Lang, a world-famous restaurateur, forged yet another success story. Lang and a partner, Ronald S. Lauder, U.S.

ambassador to Austria under Ronald Reagan and son of Hungarian-American cosmetics magnate Estée Lauder, spent $10 million to buy and renovate a decrepit turn-of-the-century restaurant in Budapest. Today, the restaurant—named Gundel—is again one of the city's most exclusive, and expensive, dining places.

The lure of fortunes—or at least easy profits—turned Hungary into a kind of captialist Old West in the late 1980s and early 1990s. The business atmosphere in the country was freewheeling, heady and optimistic. Some of the entrepreneurs, such as Petrenko and Szeles, received government help to launch their private business empires. Others, like Zwack, entered into partnerships with foreign companies (such arrangements are known as joint ventures). Still others, like Lang and Lauder, were wealthy enough to use their own capital to finance their investments.

But by far most of the investment capital that flowed Hungary's way came from foreign companies that purchased all or part of Hungarian companies. For a while, Hungary was a foreign-investment paradise. Then things turned sour.

The Foreign-Investment Strategy

The reformed Communists of the Hungarian Socialist Workers' Party and their successors, the Hungarian Democratic Forum, both believed initially that foreign investment would be the key to a successful transition to a market economy. The Communists encouraged joint ventures and began to remove legal barriers to foreign investment. When the Democratic Forum coalition took power, in 1990, it removed most remaining barriers and announced that virtually all state-owned companies would be for sale to foreigners.

The central package of laws easing curbs on foreign investment had been passed by National Assembly in January 1989. The legislation gave tax breaks to foreign investors and allowed them 100 percent ownership of Hungarian companies.

Foreign investment was the cornerstone of privatization, or the transfer of government-owned companies to private ownership. In order to get Hungary's economy in order, the country had to cut government spending. That spending could not be reduced as long as the state-owned companies—many of which were losing tens of millions of dollars a year—relied on government subsidies.

The Budapest Stock Exchange, the first such institution in post-Communist Eastern Europe, began trading in 1990. The plan was to issue shares of both private and state companies to anyone who wished to participate. But most of Hungary's politicians did not believe Hungarian citizens alone had enough investment capital (money to invest) or faith in the new system to buy up the state companies. That is why the foreign-investment strategy came about.

The very first Hungarian government-owned company to go on the trading block had been IBUSZ, the national travel agency. Shares in IBUSZ went on sale in both Budapest and in Vienna, Austria in June 1990. The agency was one-third privatized with the investments of some Austrians.

The foreign-investment strategy envisioned a stimulated national economy with only moderate inflation (an increase in currency or credit resulting in high prices) and only a temporary heavy loss of jobs in the state-owned sector. Both the Communists and the Democratic Forum thought that a growing private sector, awash with foreign investment, would soon absorb those workers displaced from the public sector. They believed that foreign investors would modernize and streamline the Hungarian economy with a minimum of hardship to the general public.

A key goal of the government's foreign-investment stratregy was to avoid performing "shock therapy" on the Hungarian economy. Shock therapy—encouraged by some Western economists—is the practice of lifting controls on prices formerly controlled by the government in order to stimulate the production of scarce goods. The move can cause goods that were once affordable but in short supply to become unaffordable for a period of time. But the profit potential also encourages the growth of suppliers. Eventually, as more suppliers compete for consumers, the quantity of goods increases. and prices naturally fall to a point of affordability.

Shock therapy has been tried by two ex-Communist countries: Poland in 1990 and Russia in 1992. In Russia, for example, the price of smoked sausage rose to 50 rubles (45 U.S. cents) a pound from 35 rubles (31 U.S. cents) a pound. Big deal, you say? Keep in mind that the average Russian in 1992 earned the equivalent of only about $4.00 a month.

Unlike Poland or Russia, Hungary has never experienced routine shortages of goods. Even when the Communists were in power, Hungarian stores were usually well stocked. So the government saw no need for shock therapy as a tool of economic reform. Of course, Hungary had to lift its own price controls (beginning in January 1990), but it did so while playing the foreign-investment card.

No country in Eastern Europe attracted more foreign investment than Hungary between the years 1988 and the start of 1994: a total of $7 billion. In the period between 1990 and the start of 1994, the figure was $5.5 billion. In comparison, in 1990–93, Poland received about $3 billion in foreign investment; and the Czech Republic and Slovakia combined, about $2.4 billion.

Many heavyweight Western companies came to Hungary. America's General Electric Company paid $350 million to take over Tungsram, a state-owned maker of electric-light equipment. The Japanese automaker Suzuki invested $140 million in an auto plant (it was the largest Japanese investment ever in Eastern Europe). Audi, part of Germany's Volkswagen automakers, spent $200 million to open an automobile-manufacturing facility near the city of Gyoer. Alitalia, Italy's national airline, invested $77 million for a 35 percent share of Malev, Hungary's national airline. Both General Motors Corporation and Ford Motor Company of the U.S. have established vehicle plants in Hungary.

The U.S. and Germany have led the way in foreign investment in Hungary. The largest single such deal came in December 1993, when a partnership of Deutsche Telekom (Germany's state-owned telephone company) and Ameritech Corporation of the U.S. bought 30.2 percent of Matav, Hungary's state-owned telephone company. The agreement was worth $875 million.

Like that of all the other countries of the former Soviet bloc, Hungary's telephone system is primitive compared to those of Western nations. Lack of capital and access to sophisticated Western technology have held back Hungary in the telecommunications area. The partial sale of Matav seems to have solved some of those problems. One Western publication detailed Matav's struggle to improve phone service:

> Despite major improvements in its telephone system over the past few years, Hungary still lags far behind the European average of thirty telephones per 100 people. (The U.S. average is more than fifty per 100.) In 1988, Hungary had fewer than ten main-line telephones per 100 inhabitants. During the past three years, Matav pursued an aggressive construction program that considerably enhanced

telephone services and resulted in more than 300,000 new connections in the 1991–1992 period. By the end of 1992, the penetration rate had increased to 12.5 telephones per 100 of the population. Some 170,000 new lines were connected in 1993, resulting in a total capacity of 1.4 million main-line connections.3

Hungary now is getting into advanced telecommunications. Westel, a U.S.–Hungarian joint venture, has set up the first mobile cellular-phone system in the country. And Matav has outbid Poland's state telephone company to provide an optical-cable link between Russia and Western Europe. Optical cables carry telephone signals in the form of light waves.

If everything had gone as planned by the government, then an endless supply of foreign capital would have flowed into the Hungarian economy, the state sector would have disappeared, and every Hungarian would have a job.

Things did not go as planned. For every major multinational corporation that invested in Hungary for the long haul, there were many others that came in only to make a quick buck. One problem, which began as early as 1988, was "hit-and-run" investment. That happened when foreigners bought up Hungarian companies, then broke up the companies and sold off the assets. Another problem was that some foreigners bought Hungarian companies simply to eliminate competitors for their own products. Some of the first foreigners to take advantage of the liberal investment rules in Hungary were Austrians, and they got a bad reputation around the country. According to the *New York Times:*

> When Austrian companies rushed in to buy up [Hungarian] retail businesses, they were looking for markets for their own products. The Austrians pushed Hungarian goods out of the state-owned companies they bought and increased the prices for their better-produced imports. Now, families complain that food at the nationwide supermarket chain acquired by Julius Meinl, an Austrian company, is unaffordable. Clothes imported by Kleiner Bauder, the new Austrian owners of a popular apparel chain, look better but are more expensive than the old Hungarian fashions.4

Many foreign investors who came to Hungary committed to long-term investment were still surprised at how long it took them to become profitable. They had not anticipated the problems they encountered with Hungarian workers. The workers were not used to being pushed to work harder, and were suspicious of Western-style management methods. Under the Communists, even unproductive workers kept their jobs, but the Western managers were quick to reduce wages or fire workers to save money.

John Welch, the chairman of General Electric, in 1994 admitted that his company had not forseen the difficulties it would encounter when it bought Tungsram in 1990. The company's production facilities were out of date, its financial records were in disorder, and its work force was much larger than was needed. GE had to spend $200 million (in addition to the $350 million purchase price) to whip the company into shape. Tungsram only began to turn a profit in 1994. "We probably couldn't have been more naive four years ago," Welch noted.[5]

The ruling Democratic Forum, which had staked its political fortunes on the foreign-investment strategy, was rocked by criticism when the benefits were not immediately apparent. Instead of a fast economic turnaround, workers were being laid off by the thousands and companies were being closed. In many towns where the local economies depended on one or two large factories, foreign investment meant that a majority of people were unemployed or facing unemployment. Opposition parties made a political issue of what they viewed as a foreign takeover of Hungary's economy.

In reaction to the criticism, in October 1992 the government pulled back from a plan to have 50 percent of the nation's state-owned companies fully privatized by the end of 1994. Instead, it announced that the government would retain sole or partial ownership of about 100 state companies in "strategic sectors." The sectors included such nationally important areas as communications, transportation and energy. At the time of the policy change, about 8 percent of all of Hungary's companies were in foreign hands.

The policy change was a signal that foreign investment was no longer as welcome as it had been. Investors began to look elsewhere in Eastern Europe, such as Poland and the Czech Republic.

Even though foreign investment in Hungary had been a record $2.2 billion in 1993 (compared with $1.7 billion in 1992), that figure was swollen by the giant Malav deal. Without the telephone-company sale, actual foreign investment in 1993 would have been $1.3 billion, less than in 1992.

Hungary, Poland and the Czech Republic Compared

When comparing the three post-Communist countries in Eastern Europe with the largest economies, the Czech Republic appears to be in the best shape overall. Some experts attribute the country's success to the fact that, unlike Hungary and Poland, the Czechs did not put their faith in privatization through foreign investment. Instead, Czech citizens were given preference in all sales of state-owned property. The Czech Republic created a voucher system that allows groups of its citizens to band together to purchase state properties.

When the Communists were ousted, in 1989, *all* businesses in Czechoslovakia had been government owned. (Communist Hungary, and even Communist Poland, had allowed some private enterprise.) One factor in favor of the Czech economy was that most of the unprofitable heavy industries in Czechoslovakia were in Slovakia. Thus, when Czechoslovakia divided into two countries at the start of 1993, Slovakia was stuck with the burden of those industries.

Annual Systematic Changes in Eastern Europe, 1993

	Inflation	Percentage of Change in Gross Domestic Product	Unemployment
Hungary	21.1	-1.5	12.2
Poland	37.6	4.0	15.7
Czech Republic	18.2	0.0	3.5

Source: *Reason,* April 1995.

By 1994, nearly everyone was unsatisfied with the outcome of foreign investment. The government was backtracking. Opposition parties, as well as nationalists within the ruling Democratic Forum, were using the issue to hammer the government. Workers by and large distrusted it. And the investors themselves were wondering if their purchases were worth the money and headaches.

Women in traditional garb in front of drying paprika peppers. Hungary has been rocked by a scandal over tainted paprika powder. (Hungarian Tourist Board)

Direct foreign investment in Hungary amounted to only about $1 billion in 1994, a sure sign that the country was losing its attraction as an investment magnet. Laszlo Lengyel, the head of Financial Research, a Hungarian investment-advisory firm, summed up the 1994 picture this way:

> Hungary expected more results from these investments. The investors are also disappointed in the speed of the [economic] transition. They expected Hungary, as the most developed of the East European countries, to go through the changes in three years. Instead, we're in the fourth year, and there is negative growth, and we can't really see how it will stabilize.[6]

The Socialist Party (the reformed Communists of the late 1980s) came to power in Hungary in the spring of 1994. The party's base of support was the working class, particularly Hungary's left-wing trade unions. The return of the reformed Communists concerned potential Western foreign investors who were already worried about the course of investment policy.

The new premier, Gyula Horn, promised to continue economic reform. But he also promised to soften the impact of reform on workers and pensioners (retired people on fixed incomes). Horn slowed the privatization process and clashed over economic policy with key officials, including Finance Minister Laszlo Bekesi, Privatization Minister Ferenc Bartha, and the chairman of the National Bank of Hungary, Peter Akos Bod. The three officials—who were respected both by Western economists and aid donors—were committed to the policies of swift privatization and "tight money." Tight money means restricting the money supply and maintaining high interest rates in order to control inflation.

Bod, who had quarreled with Premier Horn over the tight-money policy (Horn wanted interest rates eased), resigned under pressure in November 1994. Horn fired Bartha in January 1995 in an apparent power struggle over privatization policy. Bekesi quit his post soon after Bartha's departure, complaining about what he considered Horn's political interference in the reform process.

Perhaps the most blatant example of political interference came in January 1995, when Horn rejected an agreement to sell a 51 percent stake in the state-owned HungarHotels chain to a U.S. company, American General Hospitality. The sale price, approved by the State Property Agency (the government office in charge of privatization), was to have been $57.5 million. But Horn overruled the SPA, saying that the sale price was too low. America Hospitality really was interested in acquiring one of the 14 hotels in the chain—the aging riverfront Forum Hotel in Budapest—but all 14 came as a package deal. Horn's reversal angered the U.S. company, which declined to renegotiate the agreement and dropped out of the sale.

Horn's actions created a political crisis in the country. The Socialists' junior partners in the ruling coalition, the Alliance of Free Democrats, threatened to pull out of the coalition. And, as might be expected, his actions also alarmed foreign investors. Ralph Gerson, the head of the Hungary–United States Business Council, commented: "I've heard a lot of concerns from companies interested in investing in Hungary."[7]

In an attempt to placate the Free Democrats and foreign investors, Horn in February 1995 appointed Lajos Bakros as finance minister and Gyorgy Suranyi as chairman of the National Bank of Hungary. Both men, respected experts in banking and finance, were admired in international financial circles, and both appeared dedicated to a continuation of market reforms. The appointments bought some political peace and reassured some investors, but doubts remained about Horn's commitment to a full transition to a Western-style economy. However, his actions reflected the attitudes of perhaps the majority of ordinary people. A telephone poll of over 700 Hungarians, conducted by the newspaper *Magyar Hirlap* and published February 14, 1995, found that 35 percent disapproved of foreign investment in Hungary. The same survey found that only about one-third liked foreign investment, and that 28 percent believed it was "bad, but necessary."

The Growth of Private Enterprise

The debate over foreign-investment reflects only the big picture in Hungary. While the multinational corporations played a role in the country's economy, so did small- and medium-sized businesses started up by Hungarians themselves. The majority of new businesses have been in the service sector, rather than in the manufacturing sector. According to Western economics reporter Karoly Okolicsanyi:

> Service industries . . . have boomed; new accounting firms have been established; and new tax advisers seem to have multiplied. New office space is under construction, as are facilities such as gasoline stations, which were rare under the communist regime. New banking services [such as credit cards and automatic teller machines] are being provided that have long been commonplace in the West, but would have been unimaginable in Hungary until only recently.[8]

Almos Kovacs, the vice president of the National Bank, in 1994 issued an economic assessment that noted the sharp increase in growth of private enterprise between 1990 and 1993. The assessment summarized:

> The number of private enterprises had increased from 10,000 to almost 200,000, and [the number of] private entrepreneurs and proprietorships from 200,000 to 700,00 by the end of 1993. . . . The number of joint ventures had reached 21,485 by December of that year. The government had removed obstacles to entering the market and launching new businesses, and it had scrapped price and production subsidies [to businesses]. . . . Controls on wages and the flow of capital had been lifted. Revised laws on bankruptcy and the regulation of financial institutions had created conditions that had compelled more and more inefficient businesses to leave the market.[9]

Kovacs noted that the private sector had accounted for between 45 percent and 50 percent of Hungary's gross domestic product (GDP) by the end of 1993. GDP is a key measure of a country's economic output based on the total value of goods produced by all sectors of the economy. A rise of 3 percent or more in GDP is universally considered a sign of a healthy, growing economy—provided that inflation is held in check and the growth is not being eaten away by government overspending. Hungary's GDP declined by 4.5 percent in 1992, and fell by 2 percent in 1993. But the GDP grew by at least 3 percent in 1994, reflecting a genuine economic turnaround.

Deficits have a negative effect on GDP. Thus, the 1993 Hungarian government budget deficit of 199.6 billion forints (about $2 billion) was approximately 7.5 percent of GDP. Roughly speaking, the government wiped out 7.5 percent of the national economic output by spending $2 billion more than it took in.

Land and Property Compensation

People whose property was confiscated by the Communists after 1949 were compensated under a law passed by the National Assembly in 1991. Each person with a valid claim to rural land was given the option of receiving up to 50 hectares (123 acres) or a government voucher. The voucher could be used to draw on a special compensation fund totaling $1.35 billion. As a result of the law, about one-half of the nation's arable (fit for cultivation) farmland was transferred from government ownership to private ownership.

Those with valid claims to urban property each received a government voucher worth up to $67,000. The vouchers could be used toward the purchase of privatized land, but not urban property. Urban real estate prices have soared, and $67,000 is far below the market value of most property in Budapest and other cities.

The law did not offer any relief to persons whose property had been taken away before 1949, thus excluding ethnic Germans, Jews and Gypsies. Nor did it compensate the wealthy landowners who lost huge tracts when the Communists came to power.

Currency and the Tight-Money Policy

Hungary's national currency, the forint, has moved from being nonconvertible (in the Communist era) to being partially convertible. It still does not qualify as hard currency.

The United States and the European Union jointly established a so-called forint fund to help make the currency convertible as the economy stabilizes. The forint's value is determined when measured against the U.S. dollar along with a "basket," or variety, of Western European currencies. (True hard currencies are measured individually against each other: the dollar against the Japanese yen, the British pound against the German mark, the Italian lira against the French franc, etc.)

The value of the forint is ridiculously low compared to the dollar. As of mid-April 1995, one forint was worth .0082 U.S. cents. Taken another way, if you went to a Hungarian bank, you could get 121 forints and change for each dollar you chose to exchange.

Hungarian governments are following a tight-money policy. That means they are limiting the amount of currency in circulation and keeping bank interest rates high to discourage borrowing by companies or individuals. The policy is aimed at fighting inflation, or rising prices. More money in circulation, or more borrowing, means higher prices. As prices increase, workers demand higher salaries because their purchasing power has been cut. That is known as an "inflationary spiral." The Communists had held down inflation by simply imposing government controls on wages and prices. But that is not done in a free economy except in an extreme emergency.

Hungary also has battled inflation by periodically devaluating the forint when it feels the currency is becoming overvalued. Devaluation usually is made in steps of 1 percent–3 percent against the U.S. and European currencies. Hungary has had trouble with inflation, but the situation is improving. The annual inflation rate was 35 percent in 1991, 23 percent in 1993, and it fell below 19 percent in 1994.

Labor and Social Security

In the summer of 1990, the residents of Budapest began seeing something they had never before seen: large numbers of homeless people throughout the capital. There were indigent men sleeping under newspapers and panhandling near the city's tourist attractions. There were entire families, including small children, living in the city's train stations and parks. At that time, the government estimated that there were about 20,000 "hard-core" homeless people in Hungary. (The hardcore homeless were people who had no friends or relatives who could give them at least temporary shelter.) It was unclear how many of the 20,000 were in Budapest, but they appeared to number in the thousands.

Homelessness was a shocking indication of the downside of economic reform. Most of the homeless were men who had lost their jobs in the economic transition and were unable to pay their rent. Other factors impacted on the crisis, as well. For one thing, there had long been a shortage of housing in Hungary. For another, state-owned companies had been closing worker hostels (barracks-like living quarters maintained by the companies for their employees) as a cost-cutting measure. Also, some of the homeless men were immigrants from Romania and other neighboring countries who had hoped to find work in Hungary.

Under the Communists, joblessness and homelessness had been uncommon; anyone in good standing with the party could usually find a job and some form of housing, however meager. Without anticipating the problems ahead, Hungary entered its economic transition with no system of unemployment compensation or emergency housing.

By the mid-1990s, the homeless problem had eased, though not disappeared. Hungary now has unemployment compensation, and both the public and private sectors have been building new housing. However, the new housing has not kept pace with the influx of tens of thousands of immigrant Magyars (ethnic Hungarians) from Romania and Serbia.

Unemployment continues to be a persistant problem in Hungary, as it is throughout the former Eastern bloc. In 1990, the official jobless rate had been 1.7 percent, or 79,521 people. But by early 1993, the figure was 14 percent, or 705,000 people. In the spring of 1994, about 12 percent of the work force, or 593,000 people, were unemployed.

The worst-hit workers are those laid off from heavy industries, such as steel production. They generally lack the skills to enter Hungary's flourishing service sector. And they do not have the knowledge or the capital to start their own businesses.

The average Hungarian worker took home the equivalent of $130 a month in 1990. By the end of 1995, the average monthly wage rose to about $350. However, wages have not kept up with inflation. The national minimum wage, instituted in 1992, is about $112 a month.

The post-Communist law that governs management-employee relations came into effect July 1, 1992. By law, the standard work week is 40 hours, with employers required to pay overtime if their employees work on holidays or weekends. The law requires a minimum of 20 days paid vacation for all workers. If the employees of a business are unionized, then they have a right to collective bargaining. Unionized workers also have the right to strike.

Unlike Poland, which has experienced serious labor unrest during its transition to a market economy, Hungarian workers have been quiet for the most part. The worst labor disruption occurred in October 1990, when truck drivers and taxi drivers in Budapest blocked traffic for three days to protest a 65 percent hike in gasoline prices. The government partially gave in by lowering the price increase to 35 percent.

Those workers lucky enough to have jobs receive a generous package of benefits known in Hungary as "social security." It includes free (government paid) health care, free education and guaranteed pensions upon retirement. The medical-insurance aspect of the program actually predates the Communist era: Hungary was one of the first countries in Europe to ensure that its workers had health coverage.

The Democratic Forum government not only left social-security benefits intact, it expanded them. In 1992, the Council for the Reconciliation of

Interests—a body with representatives from the government, labor unions and employers—had signed a "social contract." Under the agreement, the government vowed to increase pensions by 14 percent in return for union support for a new value-added tax (VAT). The VAT is a kind of national sales tax on goods and services. Hungary imposes levies of 6 percent or 25 percent, depending on the type of product or service. Food had at first been exempt from the VAT, but was later included at the 6 percent level.

No post-Communist Hungarian government has dared to tamper with social security for fear of unleashing union unrest. Even in the face of decreasing economic output, millions continue to be spent on the program. According to economics reporter Karoly Okolicsanyi in 1994:

> Even though Hungary's GDP has declined in the past four years by almost 20 percent, expenditures on social welfare have not. The system of social benefits, including health insurance and pensions, which was established under drastically different economic conditions, has survived essentially intact despite the political and economic changes of the past four years. The age of retirement has not been changed; it remains fifty-five for women and sixty for men. The generous three-year maternity leave remains intact, and all medical care and education are provided by the government. The cost of these benefits has been the main reason for the governments high budget deficits.[10]

Government Deficits

Uncontrolled government spending drains economic growth. Hungary has been deficit spending since the end of communism. That means that the government spends more money than it takes in.

In 1994, the central budget deficit was 321.7 billion forints (about $3.6 billion), while the general government deficit was 340 billion forints (about $4 billion). The central budget is the spending approved by National Assembly. The general government figure included additional debts, including the costs of the government borrowing from the National Bank of Hungary.The central bank lends money to the government to make up for shortfalls in the central budget. Without such loans, the government would run out money. The interest rate on government borrowing was 8.2 percent in 1994.

Unprofitable state-owned companies account for a large part of the deficit problem. First, the government has to spend money just to keep the companies in operation. Second, such companies are unable to pay their required corporate taxes or meet their mandated contributions to social-security programs. For example, in 1994, the government central budget had to pay about $1.8 billion to make up for the social-security obligations of MAV, the money-losing state-owned railroad.

Simply put, deficit spending erodes economic growth. In 1994, government deficit spending amounted to about 8 percent of Hungary's gross domestic product.

Other factors also have a negative impact on the health of the economy. They include the current-accounts deficit, foreign debt and trade imbalances. Current accounts are the money (including hard-currency cash reserves) available to the government through the central bank to pay the nation's debts. In 1993, Hungary's current-accounts deficit had been $3.5 billion. It stood at $3.1 billion as of October 1994.

Foreign Debt

Hungary's 1989 accumulated foreign debt—the amount, including interest, that Hungary owes to other countries and to foreign commercial banks—was approximately $23 billion. By comparison, that was only about one-half of Poland's accumulated foreign debt in the same year. However, the Hungarian figure was—and continues to be—the highest per capita (per person) foreign debt in Eastern Europe. Hungary has a population of less than 11 million. Poland's population is over 38 million.

Between 1989 and 1993, Hungary paid $20.6 billion in principal and interest on its foreign debt, a huge sum for so small a country. Due to additional borrowing, Hungary's foreign debt has not gone down. In fact (over the last five years) it is has risen about $6 billion. But the country is proud of never having missed a debt payment. The excellent record of debt repayment explains the willingness of nations and banks to keep lending to Hungary.

Countries that rely on continuous borrowing to fuel their economies make foreign lenders and foreign investors nervous. Compare Hungary's situation to that of Mexico in February 1995. The Mexican government devalued the peso (the national currency) and panicky foreign investors (mainly Americans) began to withdraw their investments for fear of losing money. That precipitated a downward spiral in the Mexican economy. The value of shares on Mexico's stock market plunged, and the peso almost collapsed. President Clinton decided to step in and bail out the peso with nearly $50 million in U.S. emergency aid.

Mexico, like Hungary, is heavily dependent on foreign loans to keep its economy going. At the time of the Mexican crisis, that country's foreign debt had been equal to 46 percent of its gross domestic product. Hungary's foreign debt in February 1995 had been equal to 67 percent of its GDP. In other words, Hungary's present economy—like that of Mexico and other struggling nations—is a precariously balanced house of cards. Hungary's total economic output is being eaten away by its large debt burden.

Aid and Trade

Hungary is getting outside help in the struggle to transform its economy. That help is aid from individual nations, groups of nations and international financial institutions. Some of the aid is "free," in the sense that it does not have to be repaid. For example, the United States and some Western European nations have sent experts to Hungary to advise the government and the private sector on economic matters, business and agriculture. There are U.S. Peace Corps volunteers in Hungary teaching English to the populace.

Most of the assistance is not free. Rather, it comes in the form of credit or loans with low interest—or no interest—and flexible, stretched out repayment schedules. One example of such aid came in 1990, when President George Bush granted $47.5 million in credits and loan guarantees so that Hungary could buy 500,000 tons of American grain. Hungary did not get the grain for nothing; it simply purchased it without having to pay for it immediately.

Groups of nations have given Hungary short-term loans over the last few years. The groups include the G-7 (the top seven industrial countries) and the G-24 (the top 24 industrial nations). But by far the largest amounts of aid have come from international financial institutions.

In 1990, when Hungary launched its full-scale effort toward a market economy, the central banks of the Western nations banded together to give the country a total of $280 million in short-term loans. And the Bank of International Settlements (BIS) granted Hungary $80 million in "bridge financing" (a loan to help pay off debts that are coming due). BIS is an arm of the European Union, the most important multinational economic partnership on the continent.

Hungary's most important potential aid donors are the International Monetary Fund and the IMF's affiliate institution, the World Bank. The IMF extends credit to member nations that need help transforming their economies or stabilizing their currencies. The World Bank (its official name is the International Bank for Reconstruction and Development) lends money to countries that normally would have trouble getting favorable terms from commercial banks. (The bank is known as the "lender of last resort.") The IMF and World Bank are associated with the United Nations. They are financed through contributions from U.N. member countries. Hungary became an IMF member in 1982.

IMF aid comes with strings attached. In order to get assistance, a country must meet strict limits on government spending and take prescribed steps toward a market economy. Hungary signed an agreement in February 1991 that would have given the country a total of $1.62 billion in stand-by credits. Such credits are a special fund available to a country over several years if that country chooses to use it. The IMF suspended Hungary's borrowing privileges (called "special drawing rights") in 1993 because of the government's inability to meet IMF-mandated annual budget targets. Therefore, due to its runaway public spending, Hungary has been unable to rely on IMF assistance.

Hungary has aquired World Bank loans totaling about $3.5 million since the 1980s.

Imports and Exports

Hungary's main exports are heavy machinery, food, livestock, chemicals, natural gas and raw materials (especially bauxite and coal). Agriculture exports have been hampered by changing government regulations, reduced government subsidies, legal disputes over land ownership, and scandals. One such scandal involved paprika, the spicy red-pepper powder that is a major export. Some dishonest paprika entrepeneurs were found to have mixed powdered copper with the spice in order to increase their inventories and hike their export sales.

Hungary's main imports are light machinery, transportation equipment, manufactured goods and fuel. Hungary imports oil even though it has its own small oil reserves. Hungarian oil has a high sulfur content, meaning that it requires very expensive refining to remove its pollutants. Hungarian trade problems have less to do with bad government policies than with the fact that the country has had to completely reshape its trade structure. The fall of the Council for Mutual Economic Assistance (the Soviet-bloc trade organization) in 1991 had left Hungary in a hole. The Soviet Union had been its largest trading partner.

Hungarian exports declined by 50 percent in 1991, more than even the most pessimistic observers anticipated. The most positive event of the year in the area of trade was Hungary's signing of a European Community association agreement on December 16. The 10-year pact provided for the gradual entry of Hungary into the EC (today known as the European Union, or EU). That meant that Hungary eventually would be a full partner in an economically integrated Europe.

The association agreement requires Hungary to structure its trade-related institutions and regulations to fit the prevailing standards of the EU nations. For example, EU countries subsidize some industries like dairy products and steel. In order to join the EU, Hungary's dairy and steel subsidies would have to conform to EU norms. The benefits of full membership would include reduced tariffs (taxes on imported goods) on the products Hungary exported to its EU partners. Without EU membership, Western Europe would remain partially closed to Hungarian trade.

The EU began to lift it barriers to Hungarian exports in 1992. Elsewhere, Hungary and its "Visegrad" colleagues (Poland, the Czech Republic and Slovakia; see p. 122) formulated plans in 1992 to create gradually a free-trade zone in Eastern Europe. The plan envisioned a time when there would be little or no barriers to trade among the four nations.

Trade with the West picked up 1992, when Hungary exported $10.3 billion in goods. But there was a 13 percent drop ($8.9 billion) from the figure in 1993. The 1993 decline was in part due to a decrease in the nation's agricultural exports. (Agriculture output fell in 1993, when cuts in government farm subsidies forced changes in that sector of the economy.) Hungary exported about $7 billion in goods in 1994.

Germany and Austria are Hungary's number one and number two trading partners, respectively. About 25 percent of Hungary's trade (both imports and exports) is with Germany. Austria takes about 12 percent of Hungary's exports. About 14 percent of the imported goods purchased by Hungarians are Austrian-made.

Hungary's exports have not kept up with its imports. In spite of periodic devaluations of the forint—which make Hungarian exports cheaper to buy and make imported products more expensive—Hungary has had a trade deficit every year since 1990. In 1994, the country imported about $10 billion worth of products.

NOTES

1. *"Hungary: It's Unique!,"* special advertising supplement printed in *Fortune* magazine, October 18, 1993.
2. *New York Times,* May 3, 1994, Sec. A, p. 12.
3. Karoly Okolicsanyi, "Hungarian Telephone's Landmark Privatization Deal," *RFE/RL Research Report,* February 11, 1994, p. 41.
4. *New York Times,* May 3, 1994, Sec. A, p. 12.
5. Ibid.
6. Ibid.
7. *New York Times,* February 21, 1995, Sec. D, p. 2.
8. Karoly Okolicsanyi, "Macroeconomic Changes in Hungary, 1990–1994," *RFE/RL Research Report,* July 17, 1994, p. 25.
9. Ibid., p. 22–23.
10. Karoly Okolicsanyi, "Macroeconomic Changes in Hungary, 1990–1994," *RFE/RL Research Report,* July 17, 1994, p. 25.

6

Foreign Policy and Defense

*B*y the end of 1991, Hungary was fully free of Soviet domination. No longer was its foreign policy determined by Moscow. And no longer was the country under the protective umbrella of the Soviet-bloc military alliance, the Warsaw Pact. By stepping out of the Soviet shadow Hungary revealed itself for what it was: a tiny country with little clout on the world scene. Hungarians know that the best protection is to be part of a broader scheme, an economically and militarily integrated Europe. Until that time, possibly around the turn of the century, Hungary—and the other former countries of the Soviet bloc—are very much on their own. No other nation will look out for their interests. No other nation will defend them militarily.

Hungary's attempts to join the planned unified Europe have been slow and frustrating. While it has been able to forge friendly ties with most other countries, its relations with some of its neighbors in the Balkan region

Visiting Hungarian premier Jozsef Antall (left) with U.S. president George Bush on the South Lawn of the White House in 1990. (Wide World Photos)

have been strained over the issue of Magyar minority rights. One of those neighbors is Yugoslavia, where civil war erupted in 1991 as that nation broke apart. The bloody conflict is almost on Hungary's doorstep.

Hungary would like to join the North Atlantic Treaty Organization (NATO) to guarantee its security. But until that happens, the country must protect itself. It is now reorganizing its military and reformulating its defense doctrine. These tasks are difficult because Hungary cannot afford to spend much on defense.

Hungary Looks Westward

At the close of 1990, the Soviet bloc existed in name only. While it was true that the Soviet Union still existed and that the bloc's two most important international organizations, the Warsaw Pact military alliance and the Council for Mutual Economic Assistance (Comecon), were still operating, the U.S.S.R. was losing its satellites in Eastern Europe. East Germany had disappeared in the reunification of Germany. Hungary, Poland and Czechoslovakia all had pro-Western, non-Communist governments. Communist hard-liners were out of power in Romania and Bulgaria.

Then, in the summer of 1991, both the Warsaw Pact and Comecon fell apart. With no organizations to bind it to the U.S.S.R., which itself would soon collapse, Hungary looked toward the West for new allies.

On October 18, 1991, Hungarian Premier Jozsef Antall visited Washington, D.C. and held discussions with President George Bush and other top U.S. officials. The trip marked a turning point in relations between the two countries. Not only was Antall one of the first of Eastern Europe's post-Communist leaders to come to the United States, he was the first Hungarian leader to set foot in the country in more than 50 years.

Antall was treated to all the pomp and ceremony usually reserved for a visiting foreign dignitary. Bush, in welcoming the premier to the White House, praised Hungary's political transformation. "Hungary is no longer an emerging democracy," the president said. "Hungary is a democracy."[1]

Bush did more than offer words of praise. He announced a program through which Hungary could buy $47.5 million worth of U.S. feed grain (grain used to feed farm animals) on credit. Hungary needed the assistance because its own grain crop had been damaged in a severe drought during the summer of 1990. In the past, Hungary would have turned to the Soviet Union to supply the grain. Now it relied on America.

Antall's October trip to the U.S. was the second of two events that month that would set the course of Hungary's foreign policy. Earlier, on October 2, Hungary was admitted to the Council of Europe, an organization based in Strasbourg, France. The council is a forum for discussions on political and human-rights developments in Europe. Hungary was its 24th member and the first nation from post-Communist Eastern Europe to join the council.

Hungary is also an active participant in the Organization for Security and Cooperation in Europe (OSCE). The OSCE (formerly the Conference on Security and Cooperation in Europe, or CSCE) is a multinational organization that monitors human rights and security issues. Hungary hosted a CSCE summit in Budapest in December 1994 that was attended by many world leaders, including U.S. president Bill Clinton.

Taken together, the admission to the Council of Europe and Antall's trip to America showed the world early on that Hungary was forging a new foreign policy. The new foreign policy was based on friendship with the West as opposed to subordination to the Soviet Union. The military and economic ties that bound Eastern Europe to the Soviet Union completely unraveled in 1991. In the end, the Soviet Union itself shattered into 15 independent countries. But, months before the U.S.S.R.'s collapse, the Soviets had all but lost their empire in Eastern Europe.

First, the last Soviet troops based in Hungary left for the U.S.S.R on June 19, 1991. Next, Comecon—the Soviet-bloc trading organization—disbanded on June 28, at a meeting in Budapest. Then, on July 1, the Warsaw Pact disbanded at a summit of leaders in Prague, Czechoslovakia. Only the Soviet Union had wanted to keep the two organizations alive.

Hungary was finally free of the heavy hands of Soviet military and economic control. However, that did not mean that Moscow wished to see Hungary go its own way. Even before the demise of Comecon and the Warsaw Pact, Soviet leader Mikhail S. Gorbachev had pressured the new democracies of Eastern Europe to sign "friendship treaties" with the U.S.S.R. Each such agreement would provide a framework for future diplomatic, cultural and economic relations between the U.S.S.R. and the particular country. There was one major catch: Gorbachev demanded that Hungary, Poland and the other nations not join any Western organizations that he regarded as hostile to the Soviet Union.

Romania, which was not especially pro-Western, signed a Soviet friendship pact in April 1991. But Hungary, Poland and Czechoslovakia refused to sign. Their leaders regarded Gorbachev's demand as a Soviet ploy to maintain control of their countries' foreign policies. Besides, the three nations wanted to join the North Atlantic Treaty Organization (NATO), a military alliance created to counter the Soviet threat.

In the end, the resistance of the three countries forced Gorbachev to drop his demand. That cleared the way for the former Communist nations to have amicable relations with the Soviets and also be part of the new Europe. Gorbachev and Premier Antall signed a Soviet-Hungarian friendship treaty in Moscow on December 6, 1991. (Czechoslovakia and Poland also inked such agreements.) With the collapse of the Soviet Union at the end of 1991, Russia assumed responsibility for honoring the friendship pacts.

Soviet troops withdrawing from Hungary in 1989. The last Soviet forces left in June 1991. (Wide World Photos)

Russian president Boris Yeltsin paid a visit to Hungary in November 1992. Yeltsin was the first high-ranking Russian to come to Hungary since the downfall of the U.S.S.R. During the visit, Yeltsin laid flowers at the grave of Imre Nagy, the executed leader of the 1956 Hungarian uprising. Such a gesture by a Russian leader would have been unthinkable during the Communist era. Both governments were trying to end the friction between the two countries, friction that went all the way back to Russia's intervention in the Hungarian Revolution of 1848–49.

The Visegrad Summit

Hungary, Poland, the Czech Republic and Slovakia are known as the Visegrad nations, having formed an unofficial alliance based on common foreign-policy and economic objectives.

The alliance dates back to a chilly day in February 1991, when the leaders of Hungary, Poland and Czechoslovakia held a historic meeting in an ancient castle in Hungary on the banks of the Danube River. The meeting came to be known as the "Visegrad Summit," after the castle's location, the town of Visegrad. The summit was hosted by Premier Antall and Hungarian president Arpad Goncz. Those in attendance included Polish president Lech Walesa and Czechoslovak president Vaclav Havel.

The three nations were then—and are now—the most democratic and pro-captalist to emerge from the Soviet bloc. The leaders agreed to future informal cooperation in reaching the goal of integrating their countries into (in President Havel's words) "the all-European building."[2]

Stated simply, Hungary, Poland and Czechoslovakia wanted to end their decades of isolation from the rest of Europe. With that goal in mind, the leaders vowed to create a united front in pursuit of their own countries' aims. The key aim, they agreed, was to have all three countries admitted to the European Community (today known as the European Union). The union, which includes most of the Western European countries, is moving toward an economically unified continent.

Following the summit, Hungary, Poland and Czechoslovakia continued to consult with each other on an informal basis as the "Visegrad Triangle," or "Visegrad Three." When, in 1993, Czechoslovakia divided into two countries—the Czech Republic and Slovakia—the unofficial group became the "Visegrad Quadrangle," or "Visegrad Four."

U.S. president Clinton met with Hungarian president Goncz and other leaders of the Visegrad nations in January 1994, during a visit to Prague, the capital of the Czech Republic. Clinton endorsed the objectives of the alliance and praised the spirit of cooperation among the four countries.

The true significance of the Visegrad alliance is that it gives the small, relatively powerless nations—no longer part of the Eastern bloc, but not yet part of the Western world—a sense that they can direct their own destinies if they speak with one voice.

Friendly and Unfriendly Neighbors

Poland and the Czech Republic do not border Hungary, yet the three nations have very close relations. Relations between Hungary and the seven countries that surround it are, at best, a mixed bag.

Two issues—border guarantees and minorities—dominate Hungary's discussions with its neighbors. The neighbors insist that Hungary recognize the current borders and give up any claims to the lands that Hungary once ruled. On the other hand, Hungary insists that its neighbors assure the civil rights of the Magyars (ethnic Hungarians) living in those nations. Most of the 5 million Magyars who live outside Hungary reside in the neighboring countries.

Hungarian Premier Gyula Horn, who took office in 1994, stated that one of the aims of his government was to improve relations with Slovakia and Romania. Relations between Hungary and those two neighbors have been antagonistic at times. Following is a survey of the current state of relations between Hungary and its bordering countries.

Austria, on Hungary's northwest border, is perhaps Hungary's best friend in Europe. The two countries are bound by historic, cultural and economic ties that continue to this day. Austria is Hungary's second-most important trading partner, after Germany. Every year, tens of thousands of Hungarian tourists visit Austria, and tens of thousands of Austrians vacation in Hungary.

The tiny country of **Slovenia**, which was once part of Yugoslavia, is on Hungary's western border. Slovenia has good relations with Hungary in part because it was never under Hungarian domination. Hungary has never had any claims on Slovenian lands, and few ethnic Hungarians live in Slovenia. Hungary recognized Slovenia's independence from Yugoslavia in 1992.

Croatia, also once part of Yugoslavia, borders Hungary on the southwest. Hungary once dominated northeastern Croatia, a border region known as Slavonia. Croats and Magyars historically have never gotten along; however, Hungary supported Croatia's break from Yugoslavia, and gave refuge to thousands of Croats who fled the fighting in Croatia. (Hungary recognized Croatia's independence in 1992.) Today relations between the two countries might be described as lukewarm.

The republics of Serbia and Montenegro make up what is left of **Yugoslavia**. The Serbian province of Vojvodina borders Hungary on the south. The Yugoslav government has curtailed the rights of the approximately 400,000 Vojvodina Magyars. More than 50,000 Magyars have crossed into Hungary from Vojvodina since 1990. Serbs and Magyars are traditional adversaries. The long-held hatreds threatened to boil over into war in 1991, when Yugoslav warplanes violated Hungarian airspace.

Foreign Minister Gyula Horn (right with wire-cutters) helps remove the barbed wire fence at the Austrian-Hungarian border in 1989. Horn would lead the Hungarian Socialist Party to victory in 1994. (Wide World Photos)

Today, the governments of Yugoslavia and Hungary are barely on speaking terms.

Romania, to the east of Hungary, is another historic enemy of Hungary. Relations between the two nations have barely improved since 1988–90, when they nearly went to war over the mistreatment of Magyars in Romania's Transylvania region. According to Hungary there are close to 2 million ethnic Hungarians in Romania, but Romania holds the figure to be less than 1 million. Since 1990 nearly 40,000 Magyars have left Romania for Hungary. In 1992, the Romanian government reached an agreement with ethnic Hungarians in Transylvania to share power at the local level, but the pact fell apart in 1993. To this day, nationalists in Hungary call for Hungary to take back Transylvania. Although it is unlikely that Hungary would make such a move, the calls have a strong emotional appeal among ordinary Hungarians.

The former Soviet republic of **Ukraine** borders Hungary on the northeast. Hungary once ruled the border region (known as Ruthenia), and today several thousand Magyars live on the Ukraine side of the border. In 1993 Hungary and Ukraine signed a treaty guaranteeing the current border. The same pact guaranteed the civil rights of the ethnic Hungarians living in Ukraine. In spite of the treaty, some Hungarian nationalists believe that Ruthenia rightfully belongs to Hungary.

Slovakia is on Hungary's northern border. The Slovaks were under Magyar rule for nearly 1,000 years, and feelings of resentment continue to this day. About 600,000 ethnic Hungarians live in Slovakia, and they have been treated like second-class citizens by the Slovak majority. Among other things, the Slovak government has demanded that Magyars adopt Slovak-sounding names. Most Magyars have refused to do so. Slovak Premier Vladimir Meciar has been openly hostile to Hungary. The two countries maintain civil, but not warm, relations, thanks in part to their membership in the Visegrad alliance.

The War Next Door

Early in December 1995, the people of Taszar, a sleepy little village in southwestern Hungary, braced themselves for an invasion of foreign troops. Were the Russians returning? No, this time it was Americans. Far from being frightened, the bemused villagers were busy figuring out ways to cash in on the intrusion.

Taszar, the site of a Hungarian air force base, was used by the U.S. military as a staging area for the 20,000 American soldiers in the NATO Implementation Force (IFOR) in Bosnia. The purpose of IFOR was to keep armed factions separate as part of the 1995 Bosnian peace settlement. Most of the 20,000 U.S. troops, and their equipment, were transported from American bases in Germany to Tuzla, Bosnia. Taszar was a temporary stopping point en route to Bosnia.

The 2,000 citizens of Taszar marveled at the thought of so many Americans passing through their hamlet, which is located about 35 miles north of Hungary's border with Croatia. One enterprising resident, cafe owner Zoltan Tapaszti, decided to spend his life savings to stock up on American cigarettes, whiskey, and kitchen equipment to cook pizza and hamburgers. Tapaszti even named his thus-far nameless cafe the "Country Tavern" in hopes of attracting American soldiers. "If things work out well," he told a Western reporter, "this could mean a lot of money."[3]

U.S. Air Force planes began shuttling equipment into the Taszar airbase in late December 1995. Some of the pilots were dismayed at the idea of flying into a military facility of a country that a few short years ago had been considered an enemy of America.

The war in the former Yugoslav republics is practically on Hungary's doorstep. Both Croatia and Serbia border Hungary to the south, and Bosnia is only a few hundred miles south of the heart of Hungary. Thus far, Hungary has had no active role in the warfare, but it has been more than just an interested bystander.

In the late summer of 1991, fighting raged between the armed forces of Yugoslavia and those of Croatia, a republic that was attempting to break away from Yugoslavia. During the fighting, Yugoslav warplanes flew more than 20 missions through Hungarian airspace to bomb Croatia.

Hungary was neutral in the conflict, meaning that the Yugoslav military had no right to fly over Hungary to attack Croatia. The Hungarian government protested the incursions, and even placed Hungary's air defenses on alert as a warning to the Yugoslav government. It did no good; Yugoslavia continued to violate Hungarian airspace with impunity. In October 1991, Yugoslav planes on a raid over northeastern Croatia accidently dropped bombs near Barcs, a Hungarian village on the Croatian border. Yugoslav officials never even apologized for the incident.

Placing Hungary's air defenses on alert was no more than a bluff. Hungary did not attempt to force the Yugoslav planes to stay away because its aging air defenses were totally inadequate. In a military confrontation with Yugoslavia—a country with over 400 mostly modern combat planes—Hungary's tiny air force would have been overwhelmed quickly. Hungary had fewer than 150 warplanes, and most of them were obsolete. As far as ground defenses, Hungary had no modern antiaircraft missiles and its military radar stations were badly in need of upgrading. In short, an air war between the two countries would have been a mismatch. The Hungarians knew it, and so did the Yugoslavs.

Hungary was technically neutral in fighting in Bosnia. But in May 1995, it allowed NATO warplanes to transit through Hungarian airspace to attack

Bosnian Serb military positions. The decision had less to do with Hungary's dislike of the Serbs than with Hungary's willingness to cooperate in every way with NATO, an organization it hopes to join in the future. It was the Hungarian government that offered Taszar as a staging area for the deployment of American peace-enforcement troops in Bosnia—another sign of Hungary's eagerness to cooperate with NATO.

As of the start of 1996, the deployment appeared to be going smoothly. The Hungarians welcomed the American troops and, of course, welcomed the dollars the soldiers brought with them.

A Lesson in Chess

In the game of chess, the most important squares are the eight squares in the center of the chessboard. The player who controls the center squares can move his or her pieces easily from one side of the board to the other. Hungary's role in the Warsaw Pact was roughly akin to that of the center squares. Geographically, Hungary is in the center of Eastern Europe. Its chief functions in the Soviet military alliance were to guard the Warsaw Pact's supply lines and ensure the uninterrupted passage of Warsaw Pact troops between north and south. If war had broken out on the southern front (in the area of Romania and Bulgaria), for example, Warsaw Pact forces based in Czechoslovakia or Poland would have been able to move freely through Hungary to reach the front.

The Communist-era Hungarian People's Army had two principal tasks: defend Hungary (hold the center squares), and supply reserves for fighting north or south of Hungary. The Warsaw Pact never envisioned Hungary as a battleground in itself. The Soviet bloc had prepared for fighting NATO in either Germany (the northern front) or the Romania-Bulgaria southern region. The 50,000 or so Soviet troops based in Hungary were technically part of the Red Army's Southern Group.

The last Soviet troops quietly left Hungary, on June 19, 1991, with little fanfare. Soviet military bands played as the soldiers marched to rail depots around the country for the trip east. Some curious Hungarians watched them go, but the onlookers neither cheered nor booed. If there was any reaction among the Hungarians, it could be called a collective sigh of relief.

Less than a month later, on July 1, the Warsaw Pact disbanded. The two events meant that Hungary was truly free of foreign military domination for the first time in more than 40 years. But was the little country strong enough to defend its independence? The sad answer was no.

The Soviets not only had troops in Hungary, they may have had secret nuclear weapons there as well. In 1991 the former leader of Hungary's reformed Communists, Karoly Grosz, claimed that the U.S.S.R. had concealed nuclear arms in Hungary between 1956 and 1988. If true, it is most likely the weapons had been short-range (300 miles or less) "battlefield" armaments for use against concentrations of enemy troops or tanks. Grosz maintained that the Soviet leader Mikhail Gorbachev had withdrawn the weapons from Hungary in late 1988.

The Hungarian army did have some Soviet-built Scud-Bs and Frog-7s, which were medium-range ground-to-ground missiles. But those were believed to have had conventional (high-explosive) warheads, rather than nuclear warheads. Hungary began dismantling the missiles in 1990.

Hungary—unlike the Soviet Union, East Germany, Poland, Czechoslovakia or Bulgaria—never developed a military-industrial complex. That is, it never had large-scale industries that produced sophisticated military equipment. Although Hungary manufactured some small arms and light military vehicles, it never built its own planes, tanks or heavy artillery. Those weapons had been supplied by its Warsaw Pact partners, mainly the U.S.S.R. About 80 percent of all of Hungary's armaments and military equipment have come from the Soviet Union.

Defense spending was mostly secret during the Communist era. Experts believe that military expenditures hit a peak of 7.4 percent of the total government budget in 1963, and fell to about 4.8 percent of the budget by 1968. One thing is certain: Hungary's military spending—without a large military-industrial complex to feed—was relatively small compared to those of its Warsaw Pact allies.

Hungary may have had as many as 180,000 people on active duty in its army during the early 1960s, when Cold War tensions were high. By 1989, with the reformed Communists in power, Hungary's armed forces consisted of about 155,700 on active duty and over 200,000 in the reserves.

The reformed Communists in 1989 decided that Hungary's military would have to be both scaled down and modernized. The scaling down was necessary to lessen the burden of defense spending on the country's weak economy. The modernization was necessary because a time was foreseen when Hungary would not be able to depend on its Warsaw Pact allies to come to its aid in time of war. The reshaping of the military was planned to continue over six years, to be completed by the end of 1995. The governments that succeeded the Communists were committed to carrying out the military reorganization.

Reshaping the Military

By the end of 1992, Hungary's armed forces had a total of about 100,000 people on active duty. As of the end of 1993, the figure had been reduced to 78,000 (60,500 in the army and 17,500 in the air force), with about 195,000 reservists.That made the country's military the smallest in Eastern Europe, with the exception of Slovakia's defense forces (about 50,000 on active duty). The goal of the current reorganization is to have approximately 75,000 troops on active duty by 1996.

The Border Guards are also being included in the reorganization. Under the Communists, the guards had been part of the Interior Ministry—which oversaw Hungary's police and internal-security forces—rather than part of the Defense Ministry. The guards' main duty then had been to prevent Hungarians from illegally leaving Hungary. Now, they are part of the Transportation Ministry and their main duties are to prevent illegal immigration and smuggling. The 9,000 or so current Border Guards are being trained to act as a rapid-reaction force in time of war (at which time they would come under the Defense Ministry). Their job would be to set up defensive positions and hold back small units of enemy troops just long enough for Hungary's armed forces to be mobilized. Naturally, the guards, who are lightly armed, could not by themselves stop a full-scale invasion. The reorganization plan calls for about one-half of Hungary's military to be fully mobilized within the first few hours of an invasion.

Four factors are influencing the military reorganization: doctrine, arms-treaty limitations, budget restrictions and Hungary's desire to join NATO. Doctrine refers to the role envisioned for the military. Under the Communists, the old doctrine would have required Hungarians to fight on foreign soil, if necessary, in the event of a war with NATO. The new doctrine is entirely defensive in nature. It calls simply for the military to defend the homeland as best it can. In the absence of NATO membership, Hungary cannot count on any other country coming to its rescue.

The key treaty affecting Hungary's military is the 1990 Conventional Forces in Europe (CFE) agreement. The signing of the treaty, in Paris on November 19, 1990, officially marked the end of the Cold War. All of the nations of Europe, as well as the U.S. and Canada, signed the pact. The treaty set numerical limits on the military equipment and non-nuclear weapons that each country can deploy in Europe. According to Western military expert Alfred A. Reisch:

> In line with the 1990 CFE treaty, the Hungarian army has begun reducing various categories of armaments. As of July 1992, it still had 1,345 tanks (mostly the old [Soviet-built] T-34s, T-54s and T-55s, as well as some more modern T-72s) compared with the CFE limit of 835. The same situation applied to artillery pieces, which numbered 1,407 compared with the authorized limit of 840, while the 1,731 armored combat vehicles came close to the CFE limit of 1,700. The air force had 143 combat aircraft, more than 100 of them obsolete [Soviet-made] MiG-21s and MiG-23s; some modern SU-22s [fighter-bombers]; and thirty-nine MiG-24 combat helicopters—well below the CFE limits of 180 combat aircraft and 108 combat helicopters.[4]

Hungary must restrict government spending in order to have a healthy economy. That means it must put the brakes on defense outlays. But how can a strong, modern military be shaped on a limited budget?

In 1989, Hungary's defense budget had been approximately $100 billion forints (about $1.2 billion). By 1993, the budget had been reduced to 64.5 billion forints (about $750 million). For a country as small as Hungary, $750 million is a large sum of money. But, to put things in perspective, the U.S. Congress in 1992 had appropriated $755 million to pay for just some components of a single new U.S. nuclear-powered aircraft carrier. The carrier appropriation had been only a fraction of the total $253.8 billion U.S. defense appropriation for 1992. Thus, Hungary's entire 1993 military budget had been less than 0.3 percent of the sum set aside for American defense a year earlier. Hungary's post-Communist governments have had trouble holding down government spending. Therefore, defense budgets are not likely to rise significantly in the forseeable future.

Hungary has received some welcome foreign help in its struggle to reshape its military without undue spending. For example, Russia in 1993 agreed to give Hungary 28 modern MiG-28 jet fighters, plus spare parts and armor-piercing missiles (a total value of $800 million), in lieu of repaying part of a trade debt owed Hungary by the Soviet Union. It was the largest arms deal in Eastern Europe since the fall of communism.

NATO and the Partnership for Peace

Hungary was the first member of the Warsaw Pact to publicly express a wish to join NATO. But instead of NATO membership, the country has had to settle for joining in the new "Partnership for Peace."

The Visegrad Four (Hungary, Poland, the Czech Republic and Slovakia) want the protection that comes with full NATO membership. Among other things, they worry that nationalists might come to power in Russia and revive Russian aggression. Russia could not attack any single NATO member without risking war with all of the NATO states.

NATO leaders have offered several reasons why the organization cannot as yet expand to include any of the countries of Eastern Europe. One reason is that the countries are still poor by Western standards and cannot afford the financial burdens of NATO membership. (Each NATO member is required to contribute millions of dollars a year to maintain the alliance.) Secondly, the organization is wary of taking on new defense commitments in the wake of the end of the Cold War. If, for example, Hungary were admitted and a border dispute with Romania erupted into war, then all of the NATO nations could be drawn into the conflict.

But the main reason why NATO will not yet accept the former Communist nations as members is Russia's firm opposition to such a move. NATO had been founded as an anti-Soviet organization. Therefore, Russia would regard a NATO expansion to the very borders of the former U.S.S.R. as a possible threat to its own security.

The Partnership for Peace is a compromise first suggested by U.S. president Clinton and accepted by NATO. Under Clinton's plan, ex-Communist countries could enjoy some of the benefits of NATO membership without actually joining NATO, and without receiving any NATO security guarantees.

Hungary, Poland, the Czech Republic and Slovakia formally joined the Partnership for Peace early in 1994, after their appeals for NATO membership had been spurned. Russia reluctantly joined the partnership in June 1994. Russia's addition brought the number of nations in the partnership to 37 (the 16 NATO countries plus 21 former Communist nations, including all 15 of the now-independent former Soviet republics).

The partnership allows exchanges of military information, joint training exercises and other forms of cooperation among its members. Most of the 21 non-NATO members do not want to enter NATO. However, the Visegrad Four view their own participation in the partnership as a first step toward full NATO membership. Although the NATO leaders privately agree that the four will eventually be admitted to the alliance, no timetable has been set.

Life in the Hungarian Military

All young men in Hungary are subject to the military draft upon turning age 18. The draft is held twice a year. One year of military service is mandatory.

Youths who want a military career do not expect high pay or high prestige. Under communism, many Hungarians regarded the military as a tool of the Soviet occupation forces. The army was mainly a refuge for youths who lacked the education, job skills or Communist Party connections to get better employment. Now, with growing government-sector layoffs in Hungary, the military attracts those volunteers who are desperate for any kind of job. But the new defense doctrine is shrinking, rather than expanding, the number of career slots in armed forces.

Mental and physical standards for both recruits and draftees are higher now than in the Communist era. Each year since 1990, about 25 percent of all potential conscripts are rejected as unsuitable for military service.

The reorganization of the military has meant modest pay raises for officers and NCOs (noncommissioned officers) as an incentive to keep experienced leaders from leaving the armed services. (Nearly 7,000 officers and NCOs left the armed forces in the early 1990s.) Even with the pay hikes, most military personnel, including officers, continue to live and work in squalid conditions. Military expert Reisch noted:

The average monthly gross salary of officers in 1992 was 37,300 forint ($430), 3,500 forint more than in 1991, and that of NCOs 25,400 forint ($300), 2,200 forint more than two years earlier. The average monthly gross wage for conscripts was 1,500 forint ($20), 150 forint more than in 1991. Twenty percent of the officers and 32 percent of the NCOs are unmarried and often live in overcrowded bachelors' quarters. Worse still, the average life expectancy of career soldiers is only 58.9 years compared with 64.9 for the average Hungarian male.[5]

As of 1993, almost one-third of Hungary's career soldiers lived at or below the national poverty line. Incidents of suicide, alcohol and drug abuse, and crime in the military appear to be rising. Neo-Nazi skinheads have targeted youths in the military for recruitment to their ideology. The Defense Ministry has taken some steps to ease the problems, including for the first time placing chaplains on military bases. But there is a shortage of needed military psychiatrists. Hungary is committed to changing the negative image of the military. Soldiers now are assigned to public-works projects such as helping to clean up polluted areas.

Hungarian officers used to receive advanced military training in the Soviet Union. Today they are training in the United States, Canada, Great Britain, France, Austria and Switzerland. One priority is to make the officers fluent in English in preparation for Hungary's anticipated NATO membership. English is the common language of officers of the NATO states.

Taken together, Hungary's foreign policy and military doctrine are aimed at integrating into a new, unified Europe. The country wants peace with all nations, but is preparing to defend itself should the need arise.

NOTES

1. *Facts On File World News Digest,* October 26, 1990, p. 800C2.
2. *Facts On File World News Digest,* February 21, 1991, p. 120C2.
3. *New York Times,* December 4, 1995, Sec. A, p. 3.
4. Alfred A. Reisch, "The Hungarian Army in Transition. *"RFE/RL Research Report,* March 5, 1993, p. 44.
5. Ibid., p. 41.

7

Arts and Media
---

*T*he fall of communism ushered in a new era of free expression in Hungary. No longer does the government censor the arts, bar Western films or control the print media. Today, Hungarians can watch American programs on their televsions, pick up foreign magazines devoted to any subject on virtually any newstand, and attend plays that were once banned by the authorities.

But the new freedom comes with a price tag. While Hungarian publishers can choose what they print, many are struggling to survive in difficult economic times. The country's tiny film industry has had only an equally small impact on the international film market. Television and radio are still almost entirely in the hands of the government. Art theft has become a major problem.

Literature: A Day at the Budapest Book Fair

Visitors to the 1994 Budapest Book Fair, held outdoors in Vorosmarty Square in late May, were able to browse through books at colorfully decorated booths sponsored by various publishing houses. Classical music wafted through the air, played by strategically located string quartets. Clowns and magicians put on shows for children.

Even though it was the 65th annual book fair, there was something different about this one. It was not simply the presence of a wide variety of books from North America and Western Europe. Selected books from those regions had been available in Hungary since the early 1980s, when the Communists had loosened some restrictions on foreign publications. No, the difference was that there was evidence of a revival of Hungary's robust literary tradition.

Writers

Most of Hungary's major novelists, essayists and poets have not been well known outside of the country, or at least outside of Central Europe. This was due in part to the fact that they wrote in a unique language that was rarely translated for the purpose of reaching large foreign audiences. Although some of the key literary figures' works were translated into German and the Slavic languages during the era of the Austro-Hungarian Empire, there were few translations into English, French, Spanish or Italian.

Much of Hungarian writing in the pre-Communist days was passionate and rebellious in spirit. At the heart of the most important literary works was an abiding faith in native Hungarian traditions and values as a refuge in a hostile world.

Hungary's first great literary era came in 1840–60, the heyday of rebellion against Austrian rule. It was during that period that Sandor Petoefi (1823–49) wrote fiery poems urging revolution against the aristocracy and foreign domination. Other leading writers of the period included Janos Arany and Jozsef Eoetvoes.

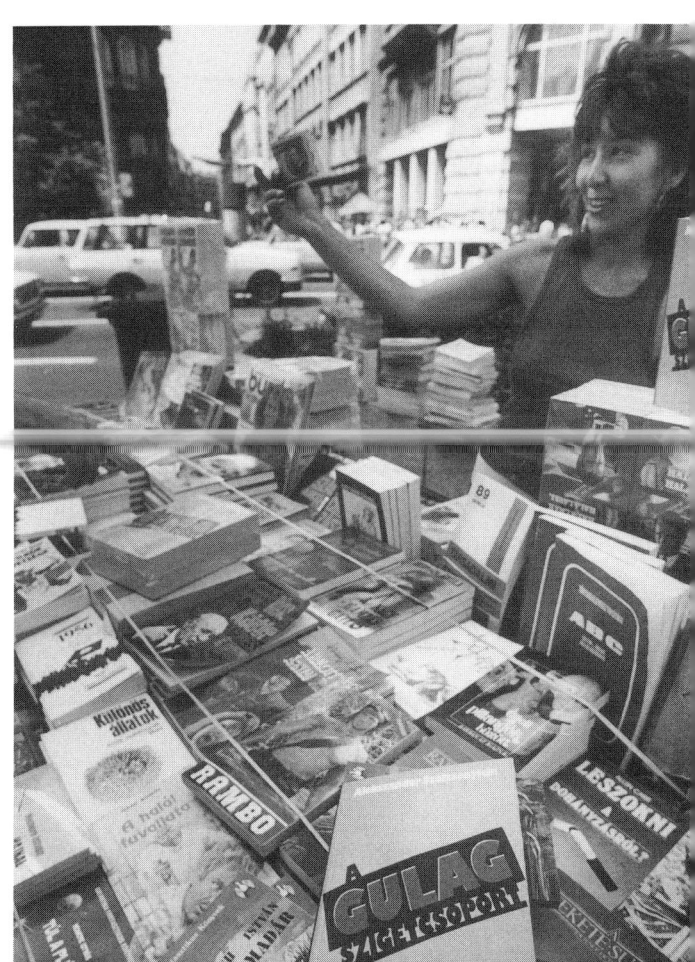

A young woman selling books at a street stand in Budapest. Once-banned works like The Gulag Archipelago *(lower center) now are freely available. Note* Rambo *(left center).* (Wide World Photos)

A second great literary period occurred at the turn of the 20th century, spurred by a group of young intellectuals associated with a pro-democracy Budapest newspaper, *Nyugat* (The West). The *Nyugat* circle included poet Endre Ady, writer Gyula Juhasz and novelist Zsigmond Moricz. Ady (1877–1919) was known for giving new life to the lyrical form of poetry. While lyrical poems were usually deeply personal, Ady used the form for political comment in the revolutionary spirit of Petoefi.

Following World War I and through the 1930s, Hungary's right-wing governments harassed the left-wing "village writers," or intellectuals who supported the peasants in their demands for land reform. Two of the best known social-protest works by the "village writers" were Imre Kovacs' *The Silent Revolution* and Geza Feja's *Thunderstorms*. Both works were banned by the authorities and their authors were imprisoned on charges of inciting revolution.

Ferenc Molnar, perhaps Hungary's most highly regarded playwright, also emerged in the period between the two world wars. Molnar was best known for his comedies, but he, too, was affected by the repressive political atmosphere. As a Jew, he emigrated to the United States in the 1930s in the face of rising anti-Semitism in Hungary.

Two major literary figures openly sympathetic to Marxism emerged during the pre-Communist days. They were poet Attila Jozsef (1905–37) and essayist/literary critic Gyorgy Lukacs (1885–1971). Jozsef's poetry featured gritty portrayals of working-class life. Lukacs gained fame for his innovative application of Marxist-Leninist social theory to literary criticism. The writings of both men were suppressed before the Communists came to power.

Several writers—including Lukacs, poets Gyula Illyes and Ferenc Juhasz, and novelist George Konrad—rose to prominence under the Communists. They were subsidized by the government and their careers were promoted by the ruling Hungarian Socialist Workers' Party. Of course, the work of those favored by the authorities was expected to be enthusiastically Marxist, or at least apolitical.

Most of the writers in good standing with Communist rulers were careful to remain so. But a few major literary figures eventually rebelled against the Communists. Lukacs was appalled by the police-state tactics of the party, became a reformist, and fell into political disfavor following the 1956 Hungarian uprising. Konrad, author of *The Visitor* and *The Founder of the State*—two novels widely hailed in Hungary—incurred the wrath of the authorities by coauthoring a study accusing the Marxist intellectual elite of being power-hungry.

A few who remained in government favor gained a measure of noteriety outside of Hungary. A lyrical poem by Ferenc Juhasz, oddly titled "The Boy Changed into a Stag Cries Out at the Gate of Secrets," was praised by the world-famous British poet W. H. Auden as one of the most remarkable poems of the post–World War II period. The poem was a mixture of dream-like fantasy and Hungarian peasant legend.

Writers who quietly opposed the government, such as poet Gyorgy Petri and film scriptwriter Sandor Csoori, found their careers blocked at almost every turn. The Ministry of Culture in 1986 accused dissident writer Istvan Csurka of "distorting history," and banned all of his works. (Csurka went on to become a leading right-wing politician in the 1990s.)

Some Hungarian writers risked fines or jail by contributing (usually under false names) articles to dissident publications. One of the best known of the underground publications was *Beszelo*, a journal started in 1979. Some above-ground magazines, like the daring literary journal *Tiszataj*, tested the limits of the censorship and lost. The government shut down *Tiszataj* in 1986 for publishing the works of banned writers.

In the late 1980s, Hungary loosened its censorship of domestic books and magazines, and began permitting some Western publications into the country. In the freer climate, cultural journals such as *Elet es Irodalom* (Life and Literature) and *Mozgo Vilag* (World in Action) flourished thanks to a growing audience of younger Hungarians. Articles in the journals, while not openly anticommunist, discussed the need for social and political reforms in ways that had not been permitted by the authorities a few years earlier.

The transition from Marxist socialism to capitalist democracy, beginning in 1989, was accompanied by lifting of the restraints on free speech. The result was an almost obsessive examination, in fiction, poems and essays, of the change. Politics and economics were the subjects of the vast majority of the works published in Hungary. While the examination was to be expected, and probably was necessary, observers reached a sad conclusion: much of what was being published was downright shallow. A key exception was the work of journalist Peter Esterhazy, who dissected the confusing post-Communist political scene in a series of acclaimed newspaper essays. But, on the whole, it was as if the years of repression had robbed Hungary's writers of their flair for innovation and rebelliousness.

An new air of optimism was evident at the 1994 Budapest Book Fair. First, there was range of new work by Hungarian writers on a variety of subjects and in a variety of styles. Second, there was strong presence at the fair of small, privately owned Hungarian publishing houses.

Browsers were treated to a fresh collection of political essays by Esterhazy, *Egy Kekharisnya Feljegyzesey* (Notes from an Intelligent

Whore), published by Helikon, one of the country's oldest publishing houses. Abovo, a small publishing house, offered a collection of short stories, titled *Horroar,* by Gyorgy Spiro, one of the new generation of Hungarian authors. As well, there was a Hungarian translation of *Under the Frog,* a novel by Tibor Fischer, a British-born writer of Hungarian heritage. *Under the Frog,* set in Hungary between World War II and the 1956 uprising, was a finalist for the 1993 Booker Prize (Great Britain's highest literary award).

Abovo was founded in 1991 by novelist Miklos Vamos. Vamos expressed some bitterness over the problems of Abovo and other small Hungarian publishers. The small houses, he said, struggled to make a profit while the large, well-established houses used their political connections to get government subsidies. "I hope the big publishing houses go bankrupt as soon as possible. The state grants go to publishers who are the favorite children of the government. The next government won't like me because I won't support them, either."[1]

Hungarians love to read, but the publishing market is limited because of the country's small population. Both large and small publishers would benefit if they could sell their books in foreign markets, especially North America and Western Europe. As of 1994, only two contemporary Hungarian writers—Peter Esterhazy and George Konrad—had had their works translated into other languages.

Tony Lang, the owner of Bestsellers, the largest English-language bookstore in Budapest, believes that U.S. publishers are missing a golden opportunity by not making deals to publish English-language versions of Hungarian books. "The publishers could exploit the audience in the United States who are second- and third-generation Hungarians who would prefer to read their Hungarian literature in English. But that takes effort."[2]

"The Vig" Reopens

On a cool October evening, the cream of Budapest society gathered at an ornate theater for a gala performance of a musical, *Ossztanc* (Let's Dance Together). Some of the theatergoers arrived in chauffered limosines, while others drove up in high-priced sedans. The men were dressed in formal attire, the women in expensive evening gowns from top French and Italian designers. A mood of quiet excitement filled the air.

A scene from the opulent pre-Communist past? No, this was 1994, and the occasion was the reopening of the restored Vigszinhas, one of Budapest's most famous theaters. The event signaled nothing less than the reawakening of theater in Hungary.

Vigszinhas roughly translates to "house of comedy." To the people of Budapest, it has always been known as "the Vig." The theater, designed by two German architects, first opened in 1896, during the period of the Austro-Hungarian Empire. It became the creative home of Hungary's most renowned playwright, Ferenc Molnar. Molnar was best known for his comedies and social satires. His very first play, *The Doctor*, had debuted at the Vig in 1902. His lone dramatic play, *Lilliom* (the basis of the American musical *Carousel*), premiered at the Vig in 1909. Molnar was the theater's resident playwright until the 1930s, when he left Hungary in fear of the country's growing Fascist movement.

In its prime, the Vigszinhas was a symbol of the golden age of Hungarian culture, the late 19th century and the early years of the 20th century. Its interior was one of the most splendid examples of baroque architecture in Central Europe. The baroque style—which dominated European art, architecture and music from the 17th century until the mid-18th century—was defined by its dynamism and extravagance. The orginal Vig had inlaid-marble floors, gold-trimmed fixtures, crystal chandeliers and seats padded in red velvet.

The Vigszinhas was badly damaged in the 1944 bombing of Budapest during World War II. The Communists rebuilt the theater and reopened it under a new name in 1951, as part of a Hungarian celebration of the birthday of Soviet leader Joseph Stalin. Needless to say, they got rid of the theater's glittering baroque elegance, which Marxists viewed as a signature of a decadent era. Under the Communists, the renamed Vig presented mainly boring dramas about the struggle of the working class. As a *New York Times* reporter observed:

> Officially called the Hungarian Popular Army Theater, it was for decades a beacon of Stalinist social realism, with boxes that were far from plush, military motifs on the walls and lighting that consisted of bare bulbs, not chandeliers.[3]

In the 1960s, when the Communists took the first cautious steps toward easing the heavy hand of censorship, a few works by Molnar were allowed to be presented at the Vig, as well as selected plays by foreign writers like Germany's Bertolt Brecht and America's Arthur Miller. But the theater itself remained a musty shadow of its former self. Ironically, by the close of the 1980s—when most censorship had been lifted—the Vig itself had fallen into disrepair.

With the end of communism in 1990, the government made a decision to restore the Viszinhas to its baroque splendor at an eventual cost of $20 million. The effort was spearheaded by Budapest's mayor, Gabor Demszky, and the Vig's director, Laszlo Marton. Even as the building was being renovated, Marton set a new creative direction for the theater. He presented plays by young Hungarian writers and staged popular foreign productions, such as the American musical *West Side Story*.

The renovation of the Vig coincided with a government drive to clean up and restore many of the old, neglected public buildings in the Hungarian capital. However, it was the reopening of the restored Vigszinhas that most symbolized a national cultural re-emergence. "This [opening night] production gives us all a chance to send a very special message," said Marton. "Theater is back."[4]

Classical Music: The Next Generation

In the fall of 1996, Hungary is scheduled to become the permanent home of a unique institution, the European Mozart Foundation. The foundation is a special school for young adults gifted in classical music. Each year since the early 1990s, about 50 students are chosen by a panel of experts to attend the school under full scholarship. The students are given a one-year intensive course in such areas as instrumentation, voice, composing and conducting.

The students come from both Eastern and Western Europe. But the foundation places particular emphasis on molding students from the former Communist countries into budding classical artists. Noted one American newspaper: "The Mozart Foundation is an academy devoted to the notion that more attention should be paid to the arts in Eastern Europe."[5]

The Kodaly Institute in Kecskemet is one of Hungary's leading music schools.
(Hungarian Tourist Board)

From the 1930s through the 1950s, hundreds of classical musicians, composers and conductors left Eastern Europe to escape the Nazis, World War II and then the Communists. (Among the emigres had been Hungary's own George Szell [1897–1970], one of the world's great conductors. Already well-established in Europe before the Second World War, Szell settled in the United States and gained further renown as the head of the Cleveland Symphony Orchestra.) As a result of the migration, Eastern Europe lost generations of talented musicians who could have passed down their knowledge and expertise to young people.

The first temporary home of the Mozart Foundation had been Dobris Castle, near Prague, the capital of the Czech Republic. In 1994, the foundation moved it to a site in Cracow, Poland. Currently its next and permanent location is to be Esterhazy Castle in western Hungary. The castle is under renovation.

Esterhazy Castle has an honored place in Hungarian history. It was the principal estate of the Esterhazys, one of wealthiest and most politically powerful families in Austrian-ruled Hungary. Between 1760 and 1790, the Esterhazys were the patrons of the great Austrian composer Franz Joseph Haydn (1732–1809), who lived and worked at Esterhazy Castle for most of those years. (A patron is a wealthy sponsor of an artist, composer or writer.)

Haydn was born in Rohrau, Austria, about 30 miles from the Hungarian border. Some of his compositions were influenced by the Hungarian peasant and Gypsy folk music he heard as a boy.

Hungarians are proud of their country's connection to Haydn. But they idolize three home-grown composers: Franz Liszt (1811–1886), Bela Bartok (1881–1945) and Zoltan Kodaly (1882–1967). To Hungarians, Liszt is known as Ferenc (the Magyar version of his first name), not Franz. He was the most talented pianist of his era, and achieved a popularity throughout Europe akin to that of a modern rock star. (Women were known to faint from excitement during his concerts.) He elevated the rhapsody, a romantic and free-flowing musical style, to a serious art form. His Hungarian Rhapsodies, a collection of 20 works written over several years, incorporated melodies from his homeland. Other famous compositions by Liszt include the Sonata in B Minor, the *Faust* Symphony, and Transcendental Studies (Douze Études d'execution transcendante). Liszt founded Hungary's National Academy of Music, in Budapest. A statue of the composer stands outside the academy.

Bartok—who once taught at the National Academy—is widely regarded as one of the 20th century's finest composers. He was a devotee of Hungarian regional folk music, and used the varying rythms and melodies throughout his orchestral works. Bartok's compositions include piano works such as *Mikrokosmos,* the opera *Duke Bluebeard's Castle* and the ballet *The Wooden Prince.*

Bartok had left Hungary for the United States in 1940, and he died in New York City five years later. In 1988, his remains were transported to Hungary, where he was buried in Budapest with state honors. Bartok's remains passed through three countries—Great Britain, France and Germany—en route to Hungary. All three nations held concerts of his music in his memory.

Kodaly was a renowned composer and innovative music educator. Like Bartok, he studied Hungarian folk music and melded that music into his compositions. He specialized in the suite, a form made up of a succession of short musical pieces. His best-known works include *Psalmus Hungaricus* and *Hary Janos*. The Kodaly Institute, one of nation's top music schools, is located in the central Hungarian city of Kecskemet.

Hungarians love classical music. Among the nation's classical ensembles, the the Budapest String Quartet has enjoyed an international reputation for excellence for more than 50 years. The city of Budapest, the national cultural capital, holds a spring music festival every year. The festival features concerts, operas, music-theater productions and open-air performances.

Festivals aside, some ensembles have run into money troubles in the wake of a government decision to freeze subsidies for the arts. The Hungarian Symphony Orchestra in 1993 found an unusual way to ease its money woes. It formed a special partnership with one of the foreign companies in Hungary, International Business Machines (IBM) of the United States. IBM sponsored some of the symphony's concerts in return for the right to advertise by placing the IBM emblem on the concert programs and tickets.

Looting as an Art Form

Hungarian art dealers, both public and private, for centuries were ardent collectors of works from all over Europe. The Hungarian National Museum contains the largest collection of Spanish art, including masterpieces by Goya and El Greco, outside of Spain itself. But how secure are these works? The theft of art, antiquities, rare books and religious objects is a growing problem in Hungary and the rest of Eastern Europe.

The problem was illustrated in December 1993, when thieves broke into the Budapest Jewish Museum and took 200 religious artifacts. The value of the stolen objects, some dating back to the 17th century, was estimated to be in the millions of dollars. Police said they had few clues in the case, but they believed the crime was committed by a professional gang.

Under communism, when the crime rate was low, most of Hungary's museums, ancient churches and historical sites lacked sophisticated security setups. Now, thievery is much more common, but security has continued to lag behind the sophisticated safeguards afforded valuable art works in the West. Art thieves today can easily cross borders that were once closed by communism. And they have found that they can sell their stolen goods to dishonest art dealers and private collectors in Western Europe and the United States.

Constance Lowenthal, the executive director of the International Foundation for Art Research, in New York City, regretted the impact of art theft on Hungary and the rest of Eastern Europe: "These countries are hemorrhaging their heritage. The hard currency, and a ready and unscrupulous market in the West, makes for a recipe for cultural disaster".[6] Lowenthal said that Eastern Europe was further disadvantaged because art collections in the region were poorly cataloged, making it difficult to trace them when they were stolen.

The break-in at the Jewish Museum was the largest single theft of its kind thus far in Eastern Europe. But art theft on a large scale is not new to the continent. During the Second World War, the Germans looted museums and private collections in every country they conquered. As Soviet forces were throwing back the Germans, they too pillaged European art. When the war ended, more than 2 million works of art and rare objects had vanished from Europe.

The Hungarian crown jewels—including the precious Crown of St. Stephen—vanished at the close of World War II. It turned out that the Nazis had removed them from Hungary to keep them from falling into the hands of the advancing Russian army. Then the jewels disappeared from Germany. Decades later, they turned up in a private art collection in America. U.S. President Jimmy Carter returned them to Hungary in 1978.

One of the great mysteries in Hungarian art history was the disappearance at the close of the war of 130 paintings in the private collections of two wealthy Hungarian families, the Herzogs and Hatvanys. The paintings are probably worth tens of millions of dollars at today's art prices because they were the works of such masters as Spain's El Greco and France's Edouard Manet and Pierre-Auguste Renoir.

The answer to the mystery came in January 1994, when Russian officials revealed that the 130 missing works were at an art-restoration center in Moscow. The Russians did not disclose how the paintings had gotten into their possession. Nor did they promise to return the works to their rightful owners.

Lights, Camera, Action

Hungary's tiny, but persistent, film industry took another small step in March 1995. That is when a new movie, *A Light-Sensitive Story,* debuted at the New Directors/New Films forum at the Museum of Modern Art in New York City.

A Light-Sensitive Story is the first post-Communist Hungarian film to get significant attention outside of Hungary. The film, directed by Pal Erdoss, concerns a young photographer (played by actress Erika Ozsda) who is struggling to make a living in 1994 Budapest. One scene depicts a newspaper editor rejecting her shots of people lined up outside an unemployment office. In a sly comment on the new capitalism, he tells her he will buy only photographs of frivolous subjects.

Hungarian movies usually get only limited distribution in Europe, and rarely make it to the United States. Unlike some other countries in Eastern Europe—most notably Poland and Russia—Hungarians never made many films. The Communists did not put much money into the industry. Today, with government subsidies lacking, Hungarian filmmakers have to scramble for private funding. Because motion-picture costs are high—and the Hungarian audience is small—films must have international distribution in order to make a profit.

Few Hungarian-language films have captured international attention. *The Revolt of Job* (1984), co-directed by Imre Gyongyossy and Barna Kabay, is set in 1943 and concerns an elderly Jewish couple who take in an orphaned Christian child. *Naplo* (1983) and *Diary for My Children* (1984) are both anti-Stalinist—and subtly anti-Soviet—films by director Marta Meszaros. *Naplo* won the third-place award at the 1984 Cannes Film Festival in France.

Hungary's most acclaimed director is Istvan Szabo. His earliest films were in his native language and won him a following in Hungary. They include *Father* (1966) and *25, Firemen's Street* (1973). But Szabo had to go outside of Hungary to get the financing and artistic freedom that brought him worldwide fame.

Szabo's *Mephisto* (1981), *Colonel Redl* (1985) and *Hanussen* (1989) are historical dramas largely financed by German investors and made in the German language. All three movies star Austrian actor Klaus Maria Brandauer. *Mephisto,* about a fictional German actor who boosts his career by collaborating with the Nazis, won the 1981 Academy Award for best foreign-language film. In spite of the German and Austrian partcipation, *Mesphisto* was a Hungarian production, and the Oscar was Hungary's first.

Several Hungarians gained movie fame in the United States and Great Britain. They include actress Vilma Banky (real name Vilma Lonchit), a Hollywood silent-film star in the 1920s; actor Bela Lugosi, the screen's most famous Dracula; the Gabor sisters (entertainers Zsa Zsa, Eva and Magda); and 1950s Hollywood director Laslo Benedek. Sir Alexander Korda (born Sandor Laszlo Korda), a producer/director of popular movies in the 1930s and 1940s, was the first filmmaker ever to receive a British knighthood, in 1942. Currently, the highest-paid screenwriter in America is Hungarian-born Joe Eszterhas (*Flashdance, Basic Instinct, Showgirls*).

"Dallas" Meets Budapest

Every Friday night, millions of Hungarians crowd around their television sets to watch the country's most popular program, "Dallas." Yes, these are reruns of the same show that captured high ratings on American TV in the 1970s and 1980s. "Dallas" is a soap opera about a conniving, filthy-rich Texas oil family. Who shot J.R.? Hungarians want to know.

The events in "Dallas" may be exaggerated, but they pale in comparison to the real-life political soap opera surrounding the ownership of Hungary's state (government-run) TV and radio networks. The systems are known simply as Hungarian Television and Hungarian Radio.

Under the Communists, all legal TV and radio stations in the country belonged to the government. That made it easy to censor or slant the news in favor of the government's agenda. As a result, Hungarians received only the news the Communists wanted them to receive. And the people viewed or heard only programs the authorities approved.

In 1989, with communism on the way out, parliament lifted virtually all government restrictions on media ownership. However, the law did not require the government to sell off (privatize) any of the state-owned radio or TV stations. With the Communists out of power, the Constitutional Court—Hungary's highest court—in 1992 overturned a Marxist-era law giving the government the power to supervise public (state-owned) broadcasting. But the court said that the Communist law should remain in effect until a parliament passed comprehensive rules on broadcasting ownership and the distribution of broadcast frequencies. No such law has been passed.

The upshot of all this is that the broadcast media in Hungary remains almost entirely in government hands. As in most countries, a broadcaster must have a government license to operate legally. Some privately owned local radio stations have sprung up, and local governments own about 40 cable-TV stations. Hungary receives broadcasts from Austria, Germany and Slovakia, as well as all major Western satellite feeds. But the national government owns the only Hungarian language TV and radio networks that reach the entire nation.

It would take millions of dollars to establish privately owned rivals to the government broadcasting systems. Hungarians do not have the money, but Western investors do. The problem is that outsiders have been blocked from buying into broadcasting. The Democratic Forum (the senior party of the first post-Communist government) used the specter of a foreign takeover of Hungary's broadcast media as a reason for prohibiting Western investment in that sector of the economy.

Public broadcasting in any country is vulnerable to partisan political influence unless carefully shielded. There has been little shielding in Hungary. In 1993, the government forced the resignations of the chairmen of Hungarian Radio and Hungarian Television and replaced them with men close to the ruling Democratic Forum. Over the next two years, the state-broadcasting networks fired more than a hundred reporters. The government claimed that the reporters were holdover Communists who were biased against the government. The main opposition political parties—the Free Democrats, Young Democrats and Socialists (reformed Communists)—charged that the firings were part of a move by the Democratic Forum to use the broadcasting monopoly to keep its grip on political power.

The opposition parties frequently complained of being denied equal access to the state media. They accused Hungarian Radio and Hungarian Television of mainly reflecting the views of the Democratic Forum in news and public-affairs programming. A large part of the Hungarian populace agreed with the opposition complaints. For example, the 1993–94 firings of reporters spurred large protests in Budapest and other cities.

The dispute over public broadcasting was one of the reasons cited by political analysts for the defeat of the Democratic Forum in the national elections in the spring of 1994. Under the winning coalition—the Socialists and the Free Democrats—the government appears to be more committed to fairness and objectivity in public broadcasting. But broadcasting is not yet open to Western ownership, leaving state radio and television still vunerable to political influence.

Outside of the political sphere, Hungarian broadcasting is thriving, given current limitations on state funding. (The government cannot afford to put as much into the area as it would like.) There are about 5 million TV sets in use in the country. Since 1993, approximately 50 percent of all Hungarian television programming has been domestically produced. Foreign programs (mainly European) account for 20 percent of content, and foreign films, about 30 percent. Domestic programs place special emphasis on Hungarian history and culture.

There is a government-run satellite station, Duna Television, established in 1992, that broadcasts exclusively in Hungarian for Hungarians abroad. A Western observer of the Hungarian media scene noted the station's particular importance: "[Duna TV's] goals are to present an objective view of Hungary, cultivate relations between peoples in East-Central Europe, convey Hungarian cultural values, and help minorities in neighboring countries preserve their Hungarian cultural identity."[7]

Foreign television-production companies increasingly use Hungary for location shooting. The nation offers a wide variety of architecture (both ancient and modern) and terrain, so it can double for almost any country at almost any period of history. Another key factor, of course, is that labor and related production costs are cheaper in Hungary than in Western Europe.

Hungary also is a good place to film rock videos. Pop superstar Michael Jackson and former wife, Lisa Marie Presley, visited Budapest in 1994 to shoot a video for his album *HIStory*. In the video, Jackson portrays a man who liberates an unidentified Eastern European country from the forces of oppression. Some Hungarians found the concept amusing. Others thought it insulting. Regardless of public opinion, Jackson's visit was another sign of Hungary's lively emergence from the gray years of communism.

An historical play performed on horseback at the Palace Festival in Visegrad.
(Hugarian Tourist Board)

Pressure on the Press

Unlike radio and television, most newspapers in Hungary are privately
owned. Their major difficulty is not undue political influence but trying
to survive in a new age of intense competition.

With the end of communism—and no restrictions on foreign ownership
lifted—there was a rush by Western publishers to buy stakes in Hungary's
newspapers. Australian-born media mogul Rupert Murdoch purchased 50

percent of two Hungarian tabloids, *Reform* and *Mai Nap,* in 1990, making him the first Westerner to have substantial ownership in newspapers in post-Marxist Eastern Europe. Other major Western investors followed, including the late British magnate Robert Maxwell, French publisher Robert Hersant and the German publishing conglomerate Bertelsmann.

As of 1993, Western investors owned about 80 percent of the capital assets in the Hungarian print media. The inflow of Western capital allowed aging printing plants to be modernized. The new managements brought with them Western know-how in marketing, advertising and distribution.

There is one big problem: There are not enough readers in Hungary to support a growing newspaper market. Most of Hungary's daily news-papers—there are over 30—operate at a loss. Most serious news publica-tions do not make money, but tabloid newspapers and magazines that feature celebrity news, gossip, sensationalism or nudity tend to break even or show a profit.

Some government-run and/or government-subsidized newspapers still exist, but most print publications are independently owned. However, independent publications are not necessarily free of government pressure. In 1993, the government imposed a tax on publications ranging from 1 percent to 20 percent, depending on the publication's content. Those with "violent" or "pornographic" content pay the highest taxes. The Association of Hungarian Newspaper Publications protested the levy as a violation of press freedom and sought court review. Meanwhile, newspapers belong-ing to the association refused to pay the taxes.

Polls in Hungary indicate that the people want factual, objective reporting in the press, but that is hard to come by. Journalists tend to view issues in political terms, and they take sides openly. According to one Western reporter: "Most Hungarian journalists still have difficulty separat-ing news from comment, and seem obliged to play a political role by supporting the group of their choice. A change of attitude inside the profession in order to meet Western criteria of objectivity and timeliness is likely to be slow and painful, since the Hungarian media in general are still staffed by journalists and reporters who for decades were accustomed to toe the line of one single party."[8]

The debates over press objectivity and broadcast-media ownership may linger, but there is little doubt that Hungary's press and arts are more free than those of most other former Communist countries of Europe. (Of the ex-Communist countries, only Poland and the Czech Republic rival

Hungary for freedom of expression.) The major issues concerning arts and media in Hungary have less to do with freedom than with the money needed to keep the press and cultural institutions alive.

NOTES

1. *New York Times,* June 7, 1994, Sec. C, p. 15.
2. Ibid., Sec. C, p.17.
3. *New York Times,* October 27, 1994, Sec. C, p. 15.
4. Ibid., Sec. C, p. 17.
5. *New York Times,*October 13, 1994, Sec. C, p. 15.
6. *New York Times,* April 12, 1994, Sec. C, p. 15.
7. Edith Oltay, "Hungarian Radio and Television under Fire," *RFE/RL Research Report,* September 24, 1993, p. 44.
8. Ibid., p. 53.

8

Snapshots: People and Places

Return of a Favorite Son

In late September 1995, a 14-car motorcade stopped in a small, poor village in northeastern Hungary. A tall, well-dressed man got out of one of the vehicles and was nearly mobbed by crowds of cheering, grinning villagers. The visitor was George Pataki, the governor of New York State.

The village, Aranyosapati, is the home of Pataki's grandparents on his father's side. He came to Hungary in part to meet distant relatives he had never before met. The visit was sponsored by the Hungarian

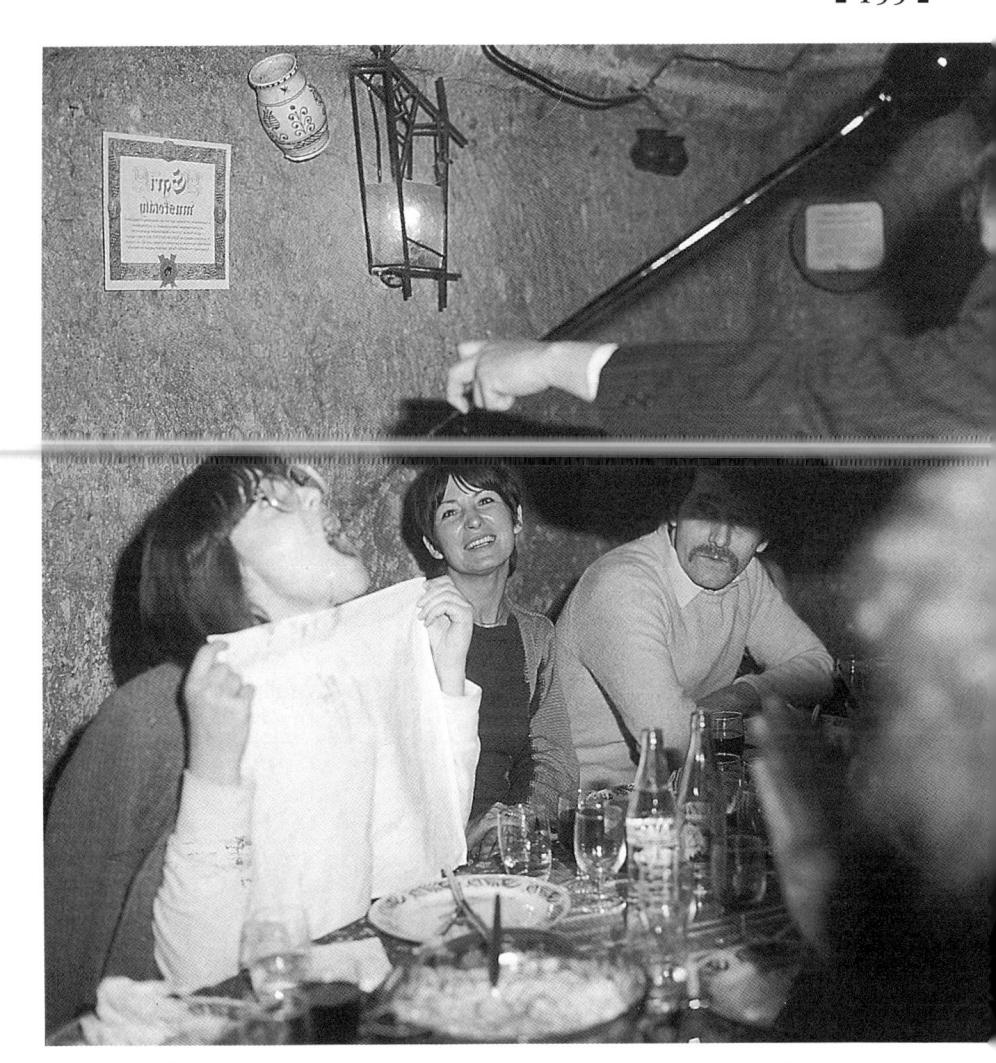

Traditional wine tasting in a Hungarian restaurant. (Hungarian Tourist Board)

government and Hungarian companies in hopes of promoting business ties between the country and New York State.

Pataki is the most prominent politician of Hungarian descent in the United States. As such, his trip to his grandparents' homeland was front-page news in Hungary. Hungarian television news crews accompanied him wherever he went.

The people of Aranyosapati—several of whom introduced themselves as the governor's distant cousins—gave him a hero's welcome.
Pataki could not resist sounding like a politician on the campaign trail.
"It's just extremely moving to look around at the crowd, and see the
faces, and know so many of you are relatives of mine," he told the
villagers. "I can tell because the women are beautiful and the men are
all handsome."[1]

School Days

A turn-of-the-century brick building in Hungary's capital houses a
daring experiment in education, the Budapest Alternative High School
for Economics. Here, most of the teachers are in their 20s and 30s.
Everyone, including the chief administrator (who has the title of
"coordinator," not principal) wears jeans, T-shirts or work shirts and
athletic shoes. Classes are small, sometimes as few as nine students.
And even though the school has plenty of desks, the teachers enjoy
sitting with their students in intimate circles on the floor to create an
informal atmosphere.

The Alternative High School has about 400 students. It opened in
1990 as an experiment in education reform. Even before the Communists came to power, Hungarian schools were both academically
demanding and strictly regimented. The one major choice offered
students was in language classes. (The national curriculum demanded
fluency in at least one language other than Magyar. Most students opted
to study German. Under communism, the curriculum required the study
of Russian.) Even though the school receives a government subsidy,
each student has to pay a tuition of $370 a year. That is slightly more
than the average monthly earnings of a Hungarian worker.

The mission of the Budapest school is excellence without regimentation. Although economics is its main focus, the school gives
its students broad leeway in elective courses and in how many
classroom hours per week they wish to devote to each course. Foreign
languages, especially English, are very popular. Orsolya Gosztony, a
26-year-old English teacher, told a visitor, "They realize they can't do

anything without languages. No one in the world speaks Hungarian except Hungarians, and the students know it."[2]

Even the economics classes are geared more to the practical—for example, how to run a business—than the theoretical. More students talk about becoming entrepreneurs than professors of economics. In the post-Communist atmosphere, they want to make Western-style big money. One 18-year-old, Andras Danko, said of his future plans, "I would like to work for an international company and then own my own company."[3]

Hungary has a long history of excellence in education, particularly in the sciences. Today the nation claims a 99 percent literacy rate. Students are required to attend school until they are 16. Admission to the country's best schools is through competitive examinations. Hungarian youngsters are introduced to such subjects as chemistry, physics, geometry and trigonometry in the elementary grades.

Products of the Hungarian education system have included Leo Szilard, the chief physicist on the Manhattan Project (the project that developed the U.S. atomic bomb), and Dennis Gabor, who won a 1971 Nobel Prize for pioneering laser holography. Hungarian-educated mathematician John von Neumann was one of the early pioneers in computer technology. Hungarian born and educated physicist Edward Teller is known as the "father" of the hydrogen bomb.

In the 1980s, an organization called the International Association for Educational Achievement tested over 200,000 students at 7,581 schools in 24 countries. One of the findings: Hungarian 14-year-olds were ahead of every other nationality in scientific literacy. Japanese and Dutch students at that age level finished second and third, respectively. American students finished 15th.

The high academic performance of Hungarian students comes with a drawback: parents and teachers put a lot of stress on the youngsters. One recent Hungarian emigre to the United States, a mother with adolescent children, surprised an acquaintance by disclosing that she was happy to have her children in an ordinary American public school. Why? Because, she explained, her youngsters are free from the academic pressure they had been under in Hungary.

The Road to Trouble

Beside a busy highway in western Hungary, near the industrial city of Gyoer, several young women stroll about in halters, miniskirts or tight shorts. Once in a while a truck or car pulls over and a young woman gets in. She will be back in the same spot in 15 minutes or so, richer by a few more forints or German marks.

This is prostitution in post-Communist Hungary. With the economic dislocation and joblessness caused by the transition to a free market, more and more young women are being drawn into this dangerous profession. One young woman, an 18-year-old high school dropout who works the Gyoer highway, revealed that she earned about $80 a day by selling herself. That is nearly the equivalent of an average Hungarian's weekly wage.

Hungary is a major transit point for trucking throughout Central Europe. Although the incidence of HIV infection and AIDS is relatively low in Hungary, there is an increasing risk that infected foreign drivers will boost the spread of AIDS in Hungary through contact with Hungarian prostitutes. According to the government, as of the fall of the 1993, there were 350 reported cases of HIV infection and 131 cases of patients diagnosed with AIDS.

The 18-year-old prostitute, named Tunde, shrugged off the danger. "There's no AIDS in Hungary," she insisted. "AIDS is only outside Hungary."[4]

Prostitution was banned by the Communists, but now it is legal. However, there are laws against profiting from prostitution, so it is illegal to be a panderer in Hungary. However, Hungarian newspapers have reported incidents of young Hungarian women being lured into prostitution in Western Europe by firms promising them high-paying regular jobs in that part of the continent.

Hungary is a major transit point for illegal drugs entering Europe from Asia and Africa. In 1994, Hungarian customs agents seized almost 1,600 pounds of heroin. Most of it had been shipped from Turkey, destined for Western Europe.

Hungarian officials are concerned about other kinds of smuggling, too. First, there is a growing traffic in Central Europe of uranium and other nuclear materials from the former Soviet states. In April 1995, Slovak agents found 37.4 pounds of uranium in a car bound for Hungary. The car carried Hungarian license plates, and three Hungarians were among nine Eastern Europeans subsequently arrested by the Slovaks.

Human smuggling, is also a problem. An undetermined number of cars and trucks traveling through Hungary carry hidden cargoes of illegal immigrants trying to get to Western Europe. Many are from Turkey, the Middle East, Africa and Asia. Hungary's Border Guards arrested close to 15,000 illegal immigrants in 1994. The Guards' spokesman, Colonel Attila Krisan, told a Western reporter, "It's like drugs—there are routes."[5]

Just as in other parts of post-Communist Europe, organized crime appears to be growing in Hungary. According to one unconfirmed figure, at least 20,000 cars are stolen in Hungary every year, most by organized car-theft rings. Most of the vehicles are shipped to other parts of Europe. (Hungarians love automobiles. They bought 88,000 cars in 1994. Germany sells more BMWs in Hungary than in any other country in Europe, excluding itself.)

Hungarians tend to believe Gypsies or the "Russian Mafia" are behind organized crime in Hungary. However, that accusation may have as much to do with anti-Gypsy and anti-Russian prejudices in Hungary than with the actual involvement of those ethnic groups in criminal activities.

The Funeral Cortege

A horse-drawn carriage winds its way along a 138-mile route between the Austrian border and the Hungarian town of Esztergom, the traditional seat of the country's Roman Catholic Church. The carriage carries a coffin with the remains of Jozsef Cardinal Mindszenty, once the Catholic primate of Hungary. As many as 50,000 Hungarians walk in somber silence behind the carriage in a line that stretches for miles. It is May 1991 and the cardinal has come home.

Mindszenty was jailed for opposing the Communists. He was released by the freedom fighters during the 1956 uprising. Then he was forced to take refuge in the U.S. embassy in Budapest when the revolt was crushed. He stayed at the embassy for 15 years, until the Communists allowed him to leave without the threat of arrest. He died in Austria in 1975. His last wish was to reburied in Hungary when the nation was no longer Communist.

Jozsef Antall, Hungary's first post-Communist premier, spoke at Mindszenty's burial in the basilica in Esztergom, praising the cardinal for his bravery and staunch faith.

Hungary has freedom of religion, but unlike the U.S. it does not have a concept of separation of church and state. The government grants small subsidies to officially registered religions. Seven million Hungarians, or about 66 percent of the population, are Roman Catholics. The Reformed (Calvinist) Church claims 1.9 million members, or 18 percent of the nation. Lutherans make up 4 percent of the country, or about 430,000 people. The center of Protestantism in Hungary is the city Debrecen, once called the "Calvinist Rome" for its citizens' staunch resistance to Catholicism.

Some Hungarians object to the government giving subsidies to controversial religious groups, such as the Church of Scientology and the Unification Church. Whatever the outcome of the debate, there is no doubt that Hungary has a colorful variety of religions, sects and cults. As one observer noted:

> [Since 1989,] the number of officially registered small denominations has grown from twenty-nine to forty-seven. Among the religious groups now registered as churches is, for example, the Federation of Hungarian Witches. It is estimated that at least thirty more sects or cults exist that are not officially registered; these include such obscure sects as the Satanists. . . . The number of believers belonging to small churches or denominations, including sects, is estimated to be 120,000.[6]

Night Life in Budapest

Budapest at night belongs to the young. For those with money, it is a night-club paradise. The partying usually does not get started until 11 P.M.

Take your pick. There is Zoldseg-Gyumoles, a hip cellar disco. There is Paris, Texas (named after a 1980 American film), a cafe that features live jazz and blues. There is the Trocadero Cafe, where the patrons play pool while drinking pina coladas. There is Marxim, a pizza joint decorated with barbed wire and Communist memorabilia. There is the Las Vegas Casino, located in the Atrium Hyatt Hotel. The casino opened in 1992, with Hollywood star Sylvester Stallone as the guest of honor.

Hungarian horseman and his steeds on the Great Plain. (Hungarian Tourist Board)

Hungary's Horsemen

In the eastern part of Hungary is the endless grassland known as the Great Plain. Here is where you find the Hungarian equivalent of the American cowboy. They are the most direct descendants of the old Magyar warriors who terrorized Europe in the ninth and early tenth centuries.

Today's Hungarian horsemen are peaceful folk, but—like their ancestors—they adore their steeds. A favorite herding trick is for one of them to stand on the back of a horse and gather the reins of several other horses and ride without falling.

The horseshoe is a good luck charm in Hungary (as in other parts of the world), but particularly so in the Great Plain region.

North of the Great Plain, in the Danube Bend region, the town of Visegrad holds a Palace Festival every year that features horse tournaments and historical plays performed on horseback.

It's in the Blood

It is easy to forget that Dracula, the bloodthirsty vampire of popular myth and entertainment, is not Hungarian in origin, but Romanian. It is true that the vampire's legendary hunting ground was Transylvania, once part of Hungary. It is also true that filmdom's most famous Dracula was a Hungarian actor, Bela Lugosi. But the historical model for Dracula had been Vlad Tepes, a brutal 15th-century Romanian prince.

Hungary, however, does have its own legendary vampire-like figure in Countess Elizabeth Bathory (1560–1614). It is said that the beautiful aristocrat kept herself youthful by bathing regularly in blood drained from the bodies of hundreds of young peasant girls murdered by her henchmen. Bathory died at the age of 54 (an advanced age by 17th-century standards), and witnesses claim that she retained an eerie loveliness up until the time of her death.

Death in Hungary

Why is the death rate in Hungary so high? Hungarian women live, on average, 73.8 years. Hungarian men live an average of 65.4 years. Those are some of he lowest such figures in Europe. Hungary's mortality rate, 13.9 per 1,000 people, is one of the highest among developed countries.

Experts attribute the high death rate and short life spans to several factors, including deteriorating living conditions, stress, high alcohol consumption, heavy smoking and pollution.

Hungary also had a stunning suicide rate: 45.5 per 10,000 during the 1980s. At the time that was the highest rate in the world. It dropped to

39.9 per 10,000 by 1990. No one has yet come up with an explanation of why so many Hungarians choose to kill themselves.

Customs, Traditions and Diversions

Hungary is a tiny nation, but it is also a fascinating mosaic of places, customs and pastimes. Here are a few that make this country unique.

Budapest has thousands of cafes and coffee shops. In those establishments, city residents have a long tradition of passing the hours gossiping, arguing over politics or playing chess while sipping coffee. However, young people are increasingly gravitating to the many American fast-food restaurants in the capital. Unlike the cafes and coffee shops, a McDonald's, Pizza Hut or Burger King has no waiters. Therefore, teenagers can hang out for hours in those establishments without being pestered to either order something or leave.

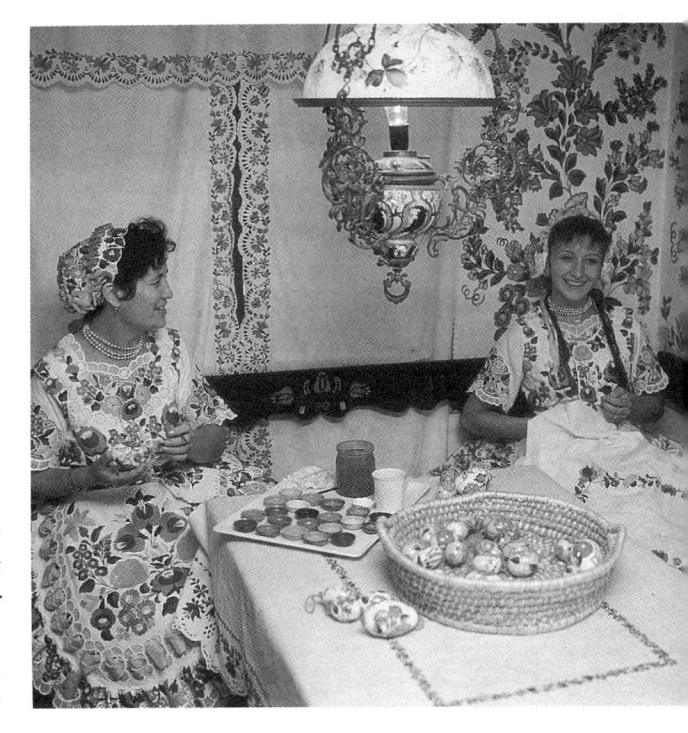

Women in traditional dress painting eggs for Easter. (Hungarian Tourist Board)

At Easter time, tradition-minded Hungarian women undertake the painstaking decoration of eggs. The painted eggs are usually exchanged between family members. In rural areas, if an unmarried young women gives such an egg to an unmarried young man, then they are betrothed. Similarly, if an unattached young man sprays perfume on an unattached young women, they are as good as engaged.

If invited to a Hungarian house for dinner, tradition dictates that the guest bring gifts to the host and hostess. What kind of gifts? A bottle of wine for the host, and flowers for the hostess. To appear at their doorstep without gifts is considered an insult.

Western Hungary, the Transdanubia region, features the Busojaras (mask festival) every year. It is a medieval tradition in which craftspeople compete to make the most frightening mask to scare away evil spirits. The festival attracts many tourists. Transdanubia also features Siklos Castle,

A crowded MacDonald's restaurant on the Pest side of Budapest. (Hungarian Tourist Board)

Siklos Castle, in western Hungary, is a major tourist attraction. It was built in the 13th century. (Hungarian Tourist Board)

one of Hungary's favorite destinations. The castle was built in the 13th century and is one of the best-preserved ancient structures in the country.

Thousands of people from all over the country travel to the Lake Balaton region to bathe in the spring waters of Heviz Lake, Europe's largest hot-water lake. The waters have legendary medicinal powers. Hungarians say their healing properties derive from the mildly radioactive (yes, radioactive) mud at the bottom of the lake.

Eger, in northeastern Hungary, is the source of a deep red wine called Bull's Blood, and the site of a castle in which 2,000 Magyars are said to have held off 100,000 attacking Turks in the year 1552. Legend has it that the defenders (led by folk hero Istvan Dobo) sustained themselves by drinking a then-unnamed wine, which stained their beards. The Turks

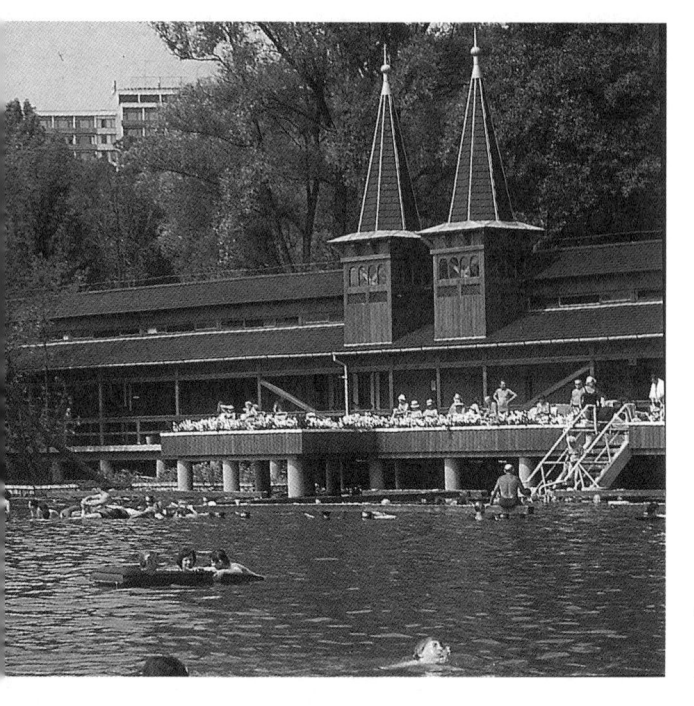

The spa at Heviz Lake has hot waters with legendary medicinal powers. (Hungarian Tourist Board)

were so impressed by the Magyars' toughness, that they believed the defenders were drinking the blood of bulls. Hungary's other most famous wine is Tokaj (Americans call it Tokay), a sweet beverage from the town of Tokaj.

NOTES

1. *New York Times,* September 25, 1995, Sec. B, p. 1.
2. *New York Times,* May 25, 1994, Sec. B, p. 9.
3. Ibid.
4. *New York Times,* September 14, 1993, Sec. A, p. 4.
5. *New York Times,* June 14, 1995, Sec. A, p. 12.
6. Edith Oltay, "Religious Sects at the Center of Controversy in Hungary," *RFE/RL Research Report,* July 16, 1993, p. 37.

Afterword: What the Future Holds

*P*resently, Hungary is just another small country in Central Europe trying to find its way in the world. It does not have the economic or military power to bully or persuade anyone. And it still has a way to go before it becomes part of the peaceful and prosperous united Europe that many envision around the start of the 21st century.

Barring unforeseen circumstances, Hungary could be a member of the North Atlantic Treaty Organization and the European Union within 10 years. For that to happen, it must stay on course. It must remain democratic and politically stable. It must take all of the painful, necessary steps toward a full market economy. And it must remain at peace with its neighbors.

The last will be no easy task, given Hungary's sometimes volatile relations with Romania, Serbia, Slovakia and Croatia. Hungary can remain at peace with its neighbors so long as those neighbors respect the rights of their Magyar populations. Mistreatment of the Magyar minorities, as in Romania and the Serbian republic of Yugoslavia, could compel Hungary to arms. (The south-central Balkan region, aflame for five years with the fighting in the former Yugoslavia, does not need any more wars.)

Statue of St. Stephen, Hungary's greatest king, in the Buda Hills. (Hungarian Tourist Board)

For now, NATO membership is but a dream. As long as Russia, with its newly energized Communists and nationalists, opposes an expansion of NATO, Hungary and the rest of the former Soviet republics will have to be responsible for their own military security. A country gets the defense it can afford, but Hungary cannot afford much. Membership in the EU for Hungary is more certain, as long as the country is willing to endure the hardships of transforming its economy.

Hungary is already a democracy, and it has suffered almost no political violence during its transition from communism. However, it does have radical fringe parties on both the right and the left. The siren call of nationalism is particularly strong on the right, which revels in recalling the days when Hungary ruled nearly all of the lands and peoples around it. Thus far, the extreme right has not had any more success in attracting mass support than its counterparts on the radical left, who yearn for a return to the good old days of totalitarian Marxism.

The economy is a much bigger and more complicated problem than political stability. After all, Hungarians want stable government, and the vast majority favors democracy over despotism. Economic reform, on the other hand, has divided the country. Hungary is now a two-tier society. Some people, most notably quick-thinking entrepreneurs, are making fortunes. Others are struggling to hang on. There is a growing middle class, while at the same time lines grow at the unemployment offices. Hungary's stores are filled with imported luxury goods, but most are beyond the pocket books of ordinary working people.

Neither of its two post-Communist governments—the conservative Democratic Forum or the leftist Socialists—has been able to control spending. Unprofitable state-owned companies continue to exist on government subsidies. Hungary's foreign debt is still much too high, although it is coming down. Inflation is being beaten, but it remains in the troublesome double digits. And now, foreign investors, who already control a large part of Hungary's economy, are looking for opportunities elsewhere in Eastern Europe.

Hungary is caught between the proverbial rock and hard place, with regard to economic reform. The push toward free-market capitalism has gone too far to easily reverse, but many more painful changes are needed to complete the transition. That means continued high unemployment and loss of purchasing power. A large segment of the population has become disenchanted with the whole process.

The economic transition reminds some Hungarians of a cynical saying that circulated throughout Eastern Europe during the heyday of communism: "We pretend to work, and the government pretends to pay us." Now, it seems, a substantial number of Hungarians cannot even pretend to work.

The future, however, is another matter. A peaceful, prosperous Hungary, in concert with its "Visegrad" colleagues has great potential. Together, the four nations have nearly 70 million people and a strong industrial base. They are already planning a Central European free-trade zone.

So, for the time being, Hungary remains in a kind of holding pattern. It knows where it wants to go. It is just not quite sure how it will get there.

Chronology of Hungarian History

The Magyars

895–896:	Magyars under chieftain Arpad invade Carpathian Basin, subjugate Slavs
896–955:	Magyars conduct raids throughout Europe
955:	Germans defeat Magyars at Battle of Augsburg
1000:	Magyar ruler Stephen crowned Christian king and holy apostle
1038:	Stephen dies, elevated to Roman Catholic sainthood
1222:	Vatican mediation ends absolute rule of Magyar kings over Magyar nobles
1241:	Mongols invade, slay half of Hungary's popuation
1301:	Last king descended from Arpad dies. Reign of non-Magyars begins in Hungary
1377:	Turkish invaders turned back at Battle of Belgrade
1458–1490:	Reign of King Matthias Corvinus. Hungary is richest kingdom in Central Europe
514:	Peasant revolt put down with large loss of life

Hapsburg Rule

1526:	Turks destroy Hungarian army at Battle of Mohacs. Most of Hungary occupied for 150 years.

	Free portion, "Royal Hungary," dominated by Austria's Hapsburg dynasty
1697:	Austria defeats Turks
1724:	Empress Maria Theresa of Austria assumes Hungarian crown
1843:	Hungarians force Magyar culture on non-Magyars living in lands ruled by Hungary
1847:	Austria grants Hungary limited autonomy
1848:	Francis Joseph becomes Austria's emperor
1848–49:	Hungary revolts against Austria. Francis Joseph gets Russian help to crush rebellion
1849–67:	Period of Hapsburg absolute rule in Hungary

The Dual Monarchy

1867:	Austro-Hungarian Empire formed. Emperor Francis Joseph, an Austrian, is also crowned king of Hungary
1914:	Austrian Archduke Francis Ferdinand assassinated, triggering First World War
1914–18:	Austria-Hungary and chief ally, Germany, defeated. Empire breaks up. Hungary proclaims itself a republic

Before Communism

1919–20:	Marxist Bela Kun proclaims short-lived Hungarian Communist state. Bloody right-wing counterrevolution follows. Period of Horthy Regency begins
June 24, 1920:	Treaty of Trianon forces Hungary to give up 87,748 square miles of territory and 13.2 million subjects. More than 3 million Magyars in lost lands come under Slavic or Romanian rule
1930–35:	Hungary draws closer to Nazi Germany and Fascist Italy
November 2, 1938:	Germany and Italy "award" Hungary a small portion of its lost lands
1939:	Second World War begins

1940–43:	Hungary formally joins Germany and other Axis powers. Hungary regains more lost territorities, but its forces are routed on Russian front
1944:	German troops aid Fascist takeover of Hungarian government. Hundreds of thousands of Hungarian Jews deported to Nazi death camps
February 13, 1945:	Soviet Red Army captures Budapest, nearly destroying city
November 7, 1945:	Free elections held. Communists finish second to Independent Smallholders
1946–48:	Communists under Stalinist Matyas Rakosi infiltrate government agencies, the military, opposition political parties and labor unions
1949:	"People's Republic of Hungary" proclaimed after the Communists merge with the ruling Social Democrats. No effective politicial opposton remains in country

Under Communism

1949–56:	Rakosi turns Hungary into a police state. Attempts at rapid industrialization fail. Hungary joins Soviet-led Warsaw Pact military alliance
October 1956:	Anti-Soviet protests in Budapest turn into bloody, full-scale uprising. Premier Imre Nagy attempts to break country from Soviet hold. Red Army smashes revolt, tens of thousands flee Hungary
1958:	Nagy, key aides executed for treason
1968–88:	Communist leader Janos Kadar institutes New Economic Mechanism. Censorship, travel restrictions eased. Hungary becomes the most liberal nation in Soviet bloc
May 22, 1988:	Kadar ousted by reformed Communists. Karoly Grosz assumes party leadership
August:	Relations with Romania sour over persecution of rural Magyars

Transitions

1989

March:	Soviet leader Mikhail S. Gorbachev vows noninterference in Hungarian political and economic reforms
May:	Hungary opens its border with Austria
June 16:	Nagy, other executed heroes of '56 uprising reburied with honors
July 6:	Former Communist leader Kadar dies
July 11:	U.S. president George Bush visits Hungary.
September-October:	Hungary allows thousands of East German tourists to receive political asylum in West Germany
October 7:	Hungarian Communists renounce Marxism-Leninism, adopt democratic socialism
October 18:	National constitution amended to allow multiparty elections. Communist political monopoly ended
October 23:	Free republic proclaimed

1990

January:	Budapest Stock Exchange begins trading. Government begins lifting state subsidies in many sectors of the economy
March 19–20:	Anti-Magyar riots in Transylvania further strain Hungarian-Romanian relations
March–April:	First truly free national elections held since 1945. Center-right coalition takes power. Jozsef Antall becomes first post-Communist premier
June:	First state-owned company, IBUSZ, privatized
October 26–28:	Gasoline price hike sparks major protests in Budapest
November 19:	Conventional Forces in Europe (CFE) treaty signed, formally ending Cold War

1991

February 15:	"Visegrad" partnership formed with Poland, Czechoslovakia
February 21:	International Monetary Fund aid pact signed

HUngary

HUNGARY
■ 174 ■

April 24:	National Assembly passes property-compensation law
June 19:	Last Soviet troops leave Hungary.
June 28:	Soviet-led trading organization Comecon folds
July 1:	Warsaw Pact military alliance collapses
October:	Hungary joins Council of Europe. Premier Antall visits United States. Hungary, Yugoslavia at odds over military aircraft incursions
December 1:	Banking system reformed
December 6:	Russian friendship treaty signed
December 16:	European Community association agreement signed

1992

| October: | Government begins to pull back on privatizing state industries |
| November 11: | Russian President Boris Yeltsin visits, honors Nagy |

1993

| December 12: | Premier Antall dies. Peter Boross heads government |

1994

January:	Western military alliance NATO rejects membership. "Partnership for Peace" joined instead
May:	Socialists (reformed Communists) win in national elections, form coalition government with Free Democrats. Socialist Gyula Horn becomes premier
December:	Hungary hosts CSCE human rights/security summit

1995

| January–February: | Socialists, Free Democrats clash over privatization, threatening political coalition |

1996

| January: | U.S. troops begin using Hungary as key staging area en route to peace-enforcement duties in Bosnia |

Bibliography

Books

Blitzer, Charles, *The Age of Kings*. New York: Time Inc., 1967.

Carter, Rowlinson, *Insight Guides: Eastern Europe*. Singapore: APA Publications [HK] Ltd., 1993.

Croteau, Maureen and Worchester, Wayne, eds., *The Essential Researcher*. New York: HarperPerennial, 1993.

Crystal, David, ed., *The Cambridge Factfinder*. Cambridge, U.K.: Cambridge University Press, 1993.

Dedijer, Vladimir, *The Road to Sarajevo*. New York: Simon & Schuster, 1966.

Dumbaugh, Kerry and Miko, Frances T., *Gorbachev's Reform Strategy: Comparisons with the Hungarian and Chinese Experience*. Washington, D.C.: Congressional Research Service (Report No. 87–813F), 1987.

Elisseefe, Vadime; Naudou, Jean; Wiet, Gaston; and Wolff, Phillippe, *The Great Medieval Civilizations—Volume III of the The History of Mankind*. New York: Harper & Row Publishers, 1975.

Enzensberger, Hans Magnus, *Europe, Europe: Forays into a Continent*. New York: Pantheon Books, 1989.

Finch, David E., *The Business Handbook to Hungary*. Budapest: Budapest Week, 1993.

Gadney, Reg, *Cry Hungary!: Uprising 1956.* New York: Atheneum, 1986.

Grant, Michael, *The Civilizations of Europe.* New York: New American Library Inc., 1965.

Grun, Bernard, *The Timetables of History.* New York: Simon & Schuster/Touchstone, 1991.

Hoensch, Joerg K., *A History of Modern Hungary, 1867–1986.* New York: Longman Inc., 1988.

Kohn, Hans, *The Age of Nationalism.* New York: Harper & Brothers Publishers, 1962.

Meras, Phyllis, *Eastern Europe: A Traveler's Guide.* Boston: Houghton Mifflin Company, 1991.

Zinner, Paul E., *Revolution in Hungary.* New York: Columbia University Press, 1962.

CIS and Eastern Europe On File. New York: Facts On File Inc., 1993.

The World Almanac and Book of Facts, 1994. New York: World Almanac, 1993.

The World Reference Atlas. New York: Dorling Kindersley Publishing Inc., 1994.

Newspapers, Periodicals and Special Publications

Facts On File World News Digest, selected issues 1975–93.

"Hungary: It's Unique!" (special advertising supplement). *Fortune,* October 18, 1993.

Hazlett, Thomas W. "The Czech Miracle." *Reason,* April 1995.

Hungaria (tourism booklets provided by the Hungarian Tourist Board), 1994–95.

Hungarian Commercial Counselor's Office, Various business/investment guides and government economic reports, 1994–95.

New York Times, selected editions 1993–95.

RFE/RL (Radio Free Europe/Radio Liberty) Report, selected issues 1993–95.

Index

Italic page references indicate illustrations and captions. Page references followed by *m* indicate maps. Those followed by *c* indicate chronology.